A Critical Study of Beethoven's Nine Symphonies

BEETHOVEN

A CRITICAL STUDY

OF

BEETHOVEN'S
NINE SYMPHONIES

WITH

a Few Words on His Trios and Sonatas, a Criticism
of "Fidelio," and an Introductory Essay on Music

HECTOR BERLIOZ

Translated from the French by Edwin Evans

Introduction by D. Kern Holoman

UNIVERSITY OF ILLINOIS PRESS
URBANA AND CHICAGO

First paperback edition, 2000
Introduction © 2000 by the Board of Trustees of the
University of Illinois
All rights reserved
Manufactured in the United States of America
♾ This book is printed on acid-free paper.

Library of Congress Cataloging-in-Publication Data
has been applied for.

P 5 4 3 2 1

CONTENTS

INTRODUCTION
D. Kern Holoman

Beethoven was the most substantial presence in Berlioz's artistic world. Beethoven fever was radiating outward from the Paris Conservatoire just as Berlioz first made his way there in late 1822 or early 1823. It was transmitted in large measure by Luigi Cherubini, who had met Beethoven in Vienna (and described him as "an unlicked bear"), and by other enthusiasts who had come to be familiar with the music. Already in 1807 the student orchestra had essayed a symphony of the intriguing "Betowen," and it is hard to imagine Berlioz not having heard the name and sensed an explosion in the making during his earliest visits to the campus in the rue Poissonnière. In late 1827 and early 1828, Cherubini and the violinist-conductor François-Antoine Habeneck organized a new faculty-student philharmonic society with the express purpose of presenting the Beethoven symphonies. The first concert of this Société des Concerts du Conservatoire featured the "Eroica" Symphony, and by the end of the first season it had presented the Third and Fifth Symphonies, the Third Piano Concerto, and the Violin Concerto, with the Sixth and Seventh Symphonies programmed for early in the second season. Flush with agitation over what he had just heard in the Salle des Concerts, Berlioz would hurry next door to the Conservatoire library for page-by-page study of the available published scores.

Beethoven's works showed Berlioz a compositional path to the *Fantastique,* largely by suggesting ways—unknown so far in the French repertoire—that the materials of symphonic discourse could be harnessed to narrative or descriptive effect. Beethovenian tactics emerged in Berlioz's music almost at once: surely that is the explanation for the astonishing leap in style that separates the *Huit Scènes de Faust* and *Cléopâtre* of 1829 from the labored, formulaic rhetoric of, for instance, the *Francs-Juges* overture of 1826. With the fourth-movement reminiscences in *Harold en Italie* (1834) and the great choral finale of *Roméo et Juliette* (1839), both modeled on Beethoven's Ninth, Berlioz showed how fully he had personalized Beethoven's rhetoric.

· · ·

Berlioz's seminal treatment of the nine symphonies and *Fidelio,* along with some remarks on the chamber music, anchors his fifth book, *A Travers Chants, Etudes Muiscales, Adorations, Boutades et Critiques,* published in 1862 by the Paris firm of Michel Lévy frères in a print run of some 1,500 copies. Most of the texts come from newspaper criticism Berlioz had written in 1837–38 for Maurice Scheslinger's *Revue et Gazette musicale*—the period and venue in which he emerged as a major journalist. They had been anthologized once before, in Berlioz's first book, *Voyage musical . . . Etudes sur Beethoven, Gluck et Weber* (1844).

Subject	Source	Reference
Music	*Revue et Gazette musicale,* 10 September 1837	C 273
Symphonies No. 1–2, 4–5	*Revue et Gazette musicale,* 28 January 1838	C 295
Symphony No. 3	*Revue et Gazette musicale,* 9 April 1837	C 245
Symphony No. 6	*Revue et Gazette musicale,* 4 February 1838	C 296
Symphony No. 7	*Revue et Gazette musicale,* 11 February 1838	C 298
Symphony No. 8	*Revue et Gazette musicale,* 18 February 1838	C 300
Symphony No. 9	*Revue et Gazette musicale,* 4 March 1838	C 301
Trios and Sonatas	*Journal des Débats,* 12 March 1837	C 238
Fidelio	*Journal des Débats,* 19 and 22 May 1860	C 886–87
"Beethoven in the Ring of Saturn"	*Journal des Débats,* 24 November 1860	C 891

Source: D. Kern Holoman, *Catalogue of the Works of Hector Berlioz,* Hector Berlioz, New Edition of the Complete Works, vol. 25 (Kassel, Germany: Bärenreiter, 1987), section C, "Feuilletons," 435–88.

A Travers Chants goes on to treat the work of the other composers in Berlioz's musical Olympus, including Gluck (*Orphée, Alceste*), Weber (*Der Freischütz, Oberon*), and Mozart (*The Abduction from the Seraglio*). And, dramatically, the book includes Berlioz's sullen article on Wagner's 1860 Paris appearances, "Concerts de Richard Wagner: La Musique de l'avenir" (The Richard Wagner Concerts: Music of the Future)—with its famous summary: "If this is the religion, a new one at that, then I am far from confessing it. I never have, am not about to, and never will. I raise my hand and swear: *Non credo!*"

The title of the book is something of a pun, indistinguishable in sound from *à travers champs:* "across the fields." The traditional English rendering is "Mid Realms of Song"; a more spirited equivalent might be "Through Fields of Song."

The present translation of *A Critical Study of Beethoven's Nine Symphonies* is the work of the British writer Edwin Evans Sr. (1844–1923), who published the Beethoven portion of *A Travers Chants* separately under this title in 1913 and offered the rest in subsequent installments.[1] Evans's English translations have previously been reprinted from time to time into the early 1970s.

Evans was a well-informed, tireless writer of popular music history and criticism, including two epochal works, *Beethoven's Nine Symphonies, Fully Described and Analyzed* (1924) and the four-volume *Historical, Descriptive, and Analytical Account of the Entire Works of Johannes Brahms* (1912–36). He was, too, the author of didactic treatises on plainchant and its accompaniment, composition, orchestration, piano accompaniment, and organ building; a translator of Wagner; and a capable organist. His son Edwin Evans Jr. (1874–1945) was also a significant music critic who championed contemporary music and was the author of an early English-language life-and-works of *Tchaikovsky* in the Master Musicians series (1906).

In his "Translator's Introductory Note," Evans offers the customary appreciation of his era for Berlioz the writer:

financially dependent on his criticism, enjoying the power of his pulpit, and profiting from his observations when it came time to compose. His essays can be compared, says Evans, with those of Schumann and Wagner, but are "characterised by a more pungent wit; and the happiness of his mode of expression very often goes far to atone for the severity of his views" (x). Evans professes "the utmost fidelity" to Berlioz's thought and spirit, though admits to having used "occasional collocations more suited to the English idiom than might have resulted from too close an adherence to original constructions" (xii).

But reading Berlioz on music he knew note-for-note is not always easy going. For one thing, the technical terminology at his disposal was barely sufficient to account for Beethovenian advances. The French is difficult, even with a score at hand, and translating with Evans's approach to achieving "utmost fidelity" in spirit occasionally results in "collocations" that are not, in fact, especially well suited to the modern English idiom. You have to recast some of the jargon into your own musical vocabulary.

Take, as an example, Berlioz's remarks about the close of the exposition in the first movement of the Seventh Symphony. At mm. 158–64, Beethoven passes through an eyebrow-raising F-major triad on his way to cadence in E major, "wrongly" taking the seventh of a subdominant F$\sharp$ seventh chord (F$\sharp$-A-C$\sharp$-E) *upward* to join unison F$\natural$s in m. 162. Today we hear and see m. 162 as a simple Neapolitan, and the "loss" of the E$\natural$ seems relatively inconsequential.

Berlioz devotes nearly three pages to this moment, writing in part:

> L'effet harmonique le plus hatement blâmeé par les partisans de la discipline scolastique, et le plus heureux en même temps, est celui de la résolution de la dissonance dans l'accorde de sixte et quinte sur la sous-dominante du ton de *mi naturel.* Cette dissonance de second placée dans l'aigu sur un trémolo très fort, entre les premiers et les second violons, se résout d'une manière tout à fait nouvelle: on pouvait faire rester le *mi* et monter le *fa dièse* sur le *sol,* ou bien garder le *fa* en faisant descendre le *mi* sur le *ré;* Beethoven ne fait ni l'un ni l'autre; sans changer de basse, il réunit les deux parties dissonantes dans une octave sur le *fa naturel,* en faisant descendre le *fa dièse* d'un demi-ton, et le *mi* d'une septième majeure; l'accord, de quinte et sixte majeure qu'il était, devenant ainsi sixte mineur, sans la quinte qui s'est perdue sur le *fa naturel.* Le brusque passage du *forte* au *piano,* au moment précis de cette singulière tranformation de

l'harmonie, lui donne encore une physionomie plus tranchée et en double la grâce.

Evans's translation reads thus:

> The harmonic effect most seriously blamed by the partisans of scholastic discipline, and at the same time the most successful one, is that of the resolution of the discord in the chord of six, five, on the subdominant in the key of E natural. This discord of the second, placed in an upper part against a loud tremolo between the first and second violins, is revolved in a way altogether new. One resolution might have allowed the E to remain, and have caused the F sharp to rise to G; whilst another might have kept the F whilst causing the E to fall to D. Beethoven uses neither one nor the other of these. Without changing his bass he brings the two parts of the discord together, in an octave on F natural, by making the F sharp descend a semitone and the E a major seventh. The chord, therefore, which was previously one of six, five, now becomes a minor sixth; its fifth having disappeared upon F natural. The sudden change from *forte* to *piano* at the precise moment of this singular harmonic transformation both gives it a more decided aspect and renders its grace twofold. (86)

In a translation of 1994, Elizabeth Csicsery-Rónay renders the passage as follows:

> The harmonic effect most criticized by the guardians of the scholastic doctrine, and at the same time the most felicitous, is the resolution of the dissonance in the six-five chord above the subdominant note [A] in the key of E-natural. The dissonant second—a very loud tremolo in the first and second violins—

is solved in a completely new way: the E could have been sustained and the F-sharp raised to G, or else the F-sharp continued and the E lowered to D. Beethoven does neither. Without changing the bass, he joins the two dissonant notes in an octave on F-natural, lowering the F-sharp a semitone and the E a major seventh. The chord of the fifth and major sixth has thus become a minor sixth without the fifth, which has vanished into the F-natural. The abrupt shift from *forte* to *piano,* at the precise moment of this remarkable harmonic transformation, heightens its distinct character and redoubles its charm. (26–27)

Not much better. What Berlioz *means* here is something like this:

> The harmonic effect most criticized by old-fashioned thinkers, and yet the most felicitous, is how Beethoven resolves the $F^\sharp$ seventh chord (ii$^6_5$ in E major) in mm. 160–61. The E-$F^\sharp$ dissonance—a very loud tremolo in the first and second violins [mirrored in the flute and oboe]—is resolved in novel fashion. Instead of having the $F^\sharp$ rise to G or the E resolve downward to D, Beethoven reverses things: the E *rises* and the $F^\sharp$ *falls,* both to $F^\natural$; and the seventh is lost. The abrupt shift from *fortissimo* to *pianissimo* at this very moment emphasizes it and redoubles its charm.

In short, such observations need some working out on the reader's part, and it helps to have the music close by.

Whatever its passing anachronisms, Berlioz's 1838 cycle of articles on Beethoven's symphonic oeuvre is arguably the first great critical treatment of that corpus in any language. To read it at a stretch is to be reminded again of how thoroughly

Berlioz's conceptual world was shaped by Beethoven: it is often as though each new sentence speaks at once of the Beethovenian subject matter at hand and its eventual reflection in Berlioz's own music.

Before the concerts at the Conservatoire, amateurs and savants alike had faltered over Beethoven's music, and now Berlioz had a hand in winning them over. The Ninth Symphony was found by one critic, Berlioz tells us, to be "not altogether lacking in ideas; but they are badly disposed and the general effect is incoherent and devoid of charm" (49–50). And if Berlioz himself was sometimes perplexed by what he heard, the puzzlement would merely send him back to the scores to seek his own explanations. There was little precedent analysis for him to read, and in Paris no Beethoven authorities were any better informed than he.

Berlioz explains Beethoven in a combination of technical analysis and emotional response—a little Eusebius, a little Florestan. Attempting to account for the wonder of the famous transition from scherzo to finale in the Fifth, he writes:

> The stringed instruments *col arco* softly take the chord of A flat, upon which they repose for a length of time. The rhythm is entirely dependent upon the kettledrums, by which it is sustained in the form of light strokes given by sponge-covered sticks; its design thus appearing in dull form against the general stagnation of the rest of the orchestra.
>
> The kettledrum note is C, and the key of the movement that of C minor; but the chord of A flat, long sustained by the other instruments, seems, on the one hand, to introduce a different tonality, whilst, on the other, the isolated *martellato* of the

kettledrum on C tends to preserve the sentiment of the original key. The ear hesitates, uncertain as to the way in which this harmonic mystery is about to issue. (65–66)

All this is true enough, and was probably accessible to a certain number of his readers. But it was the overt Romanticism of Beethoven that summoned Berlioz's best writing: "shreds of the lugubrious melody . . . alone, bare, broken and effaced" at the end of the "Eroica" funeral march, when "the wind instruments raise a cry which is the last adieu of the warriors to their companion in arms" (44); the "horrible tempest" and "awful cataclysm" of the Sixth (75); the "rainbow of melody" and "profound sigh" in the celebrated Allegretto of the Seventh (88, 89). The Andante scherzando of the Eighth Symphony he describes as "soft and ingenuous, besides being of an indolence specially graceful; like the song of two children gathering flowers in a meadow on a beautiful spring morning," and it is no coincidence that he models the *Villanelle* from *Les Nuits d'été*, where the image is of young lovers gathering wild strawberries in spring, on this very idea (96).

• • •

Altogether perhaps 20 percent of Berlioz's prose writing was collected in *A Travers Chants* and its sister volumes—*Les Soirées de l'orchestre* (1853), *Les Grotesques de la musique* (1859), and of course the *Mémoires* (1870). Although a small anthology was published in 1903 as *Les Musiciens et la musique,* it was one of the greatest of the Berliozian tragedies that by the mid-twentieth century the remainder of the *feuilletons* had been forgotten. In 1981 the excellent French music journalist Gérard Condé presented a new selection of criticism under the title *Cauchemars et passions*. The ambitious project of collecting all the *feuilletons* for publication as a complete set of at least a dozen volumes was announced in conjunction with the 1969 centenary of Berlioz's death. Volumes 1 (1823–34) and 2 (1835–36) of the work of the musicologists H. Robert Cohen and Yves Gérard had appeared by 1998. The commission overseeing the bicentenary of Berlioz's birth, Berlioz 2003, has established finishing the *Critique musicale* as its highest scholarly priority.

NOTE

1. The Beethoven essays from *A Travers Chants* were translated again by Ralph de Sola in the short volume *Beethoven: A Critical Appreciation of Beethoven's Nine Symphonies and His Only Opera, Fidelio, with Its Four Overtures* (Boston: Crescendo, [1975]). The additional portions of *A Travers Chants* were published in *Gluck and His Operas, with an Account of Their Relation to Musical Art, by Hector Berlioz* (London: W. Reeves, [1915]) and *Mozart, Weber, and Wagner, with Various Essays on Musical Subjects* (London, W. Reeves, [1918]). The entire volume was subsequently translated into English and edited by Elizabeth Csicsery-Rónay as *The Art of Music and Other Essays (A Travers Chants)* (Bloomington: Indiana University Press, 1994).

TRANSLATOR'S INTRODUCTORY NOTE.

IT was in 1828, and therefore at the age of twenty-five, that Berlioz began to take up the position of a writer upon musical subjects for several Paris journals; but from first to last the occupation was distasteful to him and never undertaken otherwise than from necessity. The principal satisfaction attending this phase of his career may probably be fixed at about the year 1834, when he became a recognised and important contributor to the "Gazette musicale de Paris," then recently founded. But even this literary connection was soon afterwards thrown into the shade by his appointment to the "Journal des Debats"; which we may fairly assume him to have found at least tolerable, since it was not until the year 1864 that he finally gave it up. It was a position which, independently of the financial help it afforded, gave Berlioz the opportunity of expatiating upon his artistic ideas; besides being probably also one of some indirect value in furthering his compositions, as a consequence of the respect in which the critic of so important a newspaper would naturally be held.

Berlioz is therefore one of the few great composers who, without pretending to eminence, have nevertheless cut a very respectable figure in the literary world. His writings, however, differ materially frcm those of the other two celebrated musicians whose dissertations have proved of such immense value to artists generally. While no less penetrating than those cf either Schumann or Wagner the criticisms of Berlioz are characterised by a more pungent wit; and the happiness of his mode of expression very often goes far to atone for the severity of his views. Moreover, though probably without actually standing for any greater earnestness on that account, his warmth of temperament is greatly reflected in his writings, their utility to the reader being thereby greatly increased. This takes the form that whatever he desires to express is so vividly pictured, so graphically illustrated and so passionately set forth, that, not only is a conviction in its favour rendered an almost foregone conclusion, but the perusal of his page is coupled with an amount of entertainment which dispenses the memory from all effort.

The leading items of Berlioz's literary output are comprised in the following list:

"Voyage Musical en Allemagne et en Italie." (Paris, 1845.)

"Les Soirées de l'Orchestre." (Paris, 1853-4.)

"Les grotesques de la Musique." (Paris, 1859.)

"A travers Chants." (Paris, 1862.)
in addition to which volumes are extant entitled,
respectively, "La musique et les musiciens," "Corres-
pondance inédite," "Lettres intimes" and "Mémoires."
There is also the treatise on instrumentation; which, in
spite of the many changes in constitution of the orchestra since the date of its production, still retains a high
degree of authority.   Of the musical merit of Berlioz,
however, we have no purpose at present to speak; but
entirely of his criticisms and specially, of course, of
those contained in the present work.

The first part now introduced is comprised princi-
pally of the review of Beethoven's symphonies and that
of "Fidelio"; with regard to the former of which it
may be doubted whether, in spite of the vast amount of
literature to which those masterworks have given rise,
any have yet appeared to depict so vividly their leading features.   It is quite safe to aver that the merit of
other literature devoted to the subject can never place
these descriptions out of date; for they can be read
with an intense pleasure even by those unacquainted
with the scores to which they refer—a singular merit
in analyses which are at the same time musicianly in
the very highest degree.   When we further reflect that
they were written at a time when Beethoven's fame
was in its infancy, comparatively, and that no subsequent criticism of the same works has revealed any flaw
in the views expressed, it is impossible not to accord to
Berlioz's judgment our very highest esteem.

The same general terms apply equally to the description of "Fidelio"; the study of Berlioz's essay being almost a necessity for any student desirous of becoming intelligently familiar with that opera. The remarks upon the smaller works of Beethoven are really in sequel to those upon the symphonies; but in "Beethoven in the Ring of Saturn" we have an excellent sample of Berlioz's wit, and one which will greatly help the reader to realise the distinction alluded to as existing between Berlioz and other literary musicians. The remaining papers are all conceived in Berlioz's lighter style; notwithstanding that there is no diminution of earnestness in the treatment of the serious subjects involved. The only one in which Berlioz can be said to allow us to forget his natural warmth of temperament is the introductory essay on "Music"; the difference in style of which is partly accounted for by the author himself, who tells us that it has been rescued from a work no longer existing, and which had been published twenty years before.

With regard to the translation the endeavour has been to enable the reader to imagine himself engaged in the perusal of an original. The utmost fidelity to thought and spirit has been preserved, but liberty is taken in favour of occasional collocations more suited to the English idiom than might have resulted from too close an adherence to original constructions.

A Critical Study of Beethoven's Nine Symphonies

MID REALMS OF SONG
(A TRAVERS CHANTS)

I.—MUSIC.*

MUSIC is the art of producing emotion, by means of combinations of sound, upon men both intelligent and gifted with special and cultivated senses. To define music in this way is equivalent to admitting that we do not believe it to be, as some say, *made for everybody*. Whatever may, in fact, be the conditions of its existence—whatever may have been at any time its means of action, whether simple or complex, gentle or energetic—it has always appeared evi-

---

* This chapter was published some twenty years ago in a book which no longer exists, and of which sundry fragments are reproduced in this volume. The reader may probably not be displeased to meet with it before proceeding to follow us in the analytical studies we are about to undertake of some celebrated *chefs d'œuvre* of musical art. (Author's note.)

1

dent to the impartial observer that a large number of persons remained incapable of either feeling or understanding its power. *Such people were not made for it;* and it follows that it was not made for them.

Music is, at one and the same time, both a sentiment and a science. It exacts from anyone who cultivates it, whether as executant or composer, both a natural inspiration and a range of knowledge only to be acquired by long study and profound meditation. It is this union of knowledge with inspiration which constitutes the art. Outside these conditions, therefore, the musician can only be an incomplete artist; even if he merits to be called an artist at all. The grand question as to which is pre-eminent, whether a natural organisation without study, or study without natural organisation —a question, moreover, which Horace did not venture to decide positively in the case of poets—seems to us equally difficult to settle in the case of musicians. We have seen some men, perfectly unacquainted with science, instinctively produce airs not only graceful, but even sublime; as, for example, Rouget de l'Isle and his immortal "Marseillaise"; but such flashes of inspiration illumine only part of art's domain, whilst other portions, equally important, remain obscure. From this it follows, due regard being had to the complex nature of our music, that these men could not be definitively classified as musicians—THEY LACK THE NECESSARY KNOWLEDGE.

It is even more common to meet with methodical

natures who are calm and cold; and who, after having made patient theoretical studies, after having accumulated observations, by bringing their mind to bear upon the subject for a long time succeed in drawing all that is possible from their incomplete faculties. Such as these manage to write things which seem, in appearance, to fulfil the conditions usually expected from music; but they satisfy the ear without charming it, and impart nothing either to the heart or to the imagination. Now, the mere satisfaction of the ear is very far removed from the delicious sensations which that organ is capable of experiencing; besides which the delights both of heart and imagination do not belong to the category of those which may be held lightly in account. And, as these are both united to a sensual pleasure of the most lively kind in all true musical works of any school, such incapable producers should also, in our opinion, be excluded from the class of those whom we estimate as musicians: THEY LACK THE NECESSARY FEELING.

What we call music is a new art; in the sense that it resembles in all probability but very slightly what the civilised nations of antiquity designated by that name. Moreover, we must hasten to mention that the word music anciently bore an acceptation of such extent that, far from merely signifying, as nowadays, the art of combining sounds, it was equally applied to dance, gesture, poetry and eloquence—even the whole collection of sciences being included within its range of meaning. If we suppose the word *music* etymologically traceable to *muse*, the wide meaning assigned to it by the ancients is at once explained. It expressed, and was evidently intended to express, *whatever was presided over by the Muses*. This accounts for the mistakes of interpretation into which many commentators of ancient times have fallen. There exists, however, in our current speech an established expression with a sense almost as general. In speaking of the union of works of intelligence, whether alone or aided by certain organs, as well as those exercises of the body which our intellect has poetised, we say: *Art*. It thus may happen that the reader who, in two thousand years, may come across titles so commonly applied in our books to rambling dissertations, such as—"On the state of Art in Europe during the nineteenth century," may have to interpret it thus: "On the state of poetry, eloquence, music, painting, engraving, sculpture, architecture, dramatic action, pantomime and dance during the nineteenth century." Evidently with the exception of the exact sciences, to which it is not applied, our word *art* corresponds very closely to the word *music* as used by the ancients.

What musical art, properly so called, was among them, we know but most imperfectly. Some isolated facts, related perhaps with an exaggeration similar to that of which we have every day analogous examples; the ideas, either bombastic or altogether absurd, of

certain philosophers; besides, in some instances, the
false interpretation of their writings; all these tended
to attribute to their music an immense power and such
an influence upon manners that legislators were
obliged, in the interest of their people, to determine
its progress and regulate its use. Without taking any
account of causes which may have contributed to adul-
teration of the truth in this respect, and admitting
that the music of the Greeks may really have produced
on some individuals extraordinary impressions—impressions neither due to the ideas expressed by the
poetry nor to either the facial expression or acting of
the singer, but really to music and to music alone—
this fact would not in any way prove that the art had
attained amongst them to any high degree of perfection. Who does not know the violent action of musical sounds, combined in the most ordinary fashion,
upon nervous temperaments in certain circumstances?
After a splendid feast, for instance, when, excited by
the intoxicating acclamations of a crowd of adorers;
by the remembrance of a recent triumph; by the hope
of new victories; by the aspect of arms as well as by
that of beautiful slaves surrounding him; by ideas of
voluptuousness of love, glory, power, immortality—
the whole enhanced by the powerful effects both of
good fare and wine; Alexander (whose organisation
moreover was so impressionable that he could fall into
ecstasy at the accents of Timothy) can easily be imagined moved somewhat powerfully, his state of

sensibility at the time being one almost amounting to ill-health, without its requiring any great efforts on the part of the singer to produce such an effect.

Rousseau, in quoting the more modern example of Eric, King of Denmark, who killed his best servants whilst in a state of frenzy caused by certain songs, calls attention, it is true, to the fact that these unfortunates must have been far less susceptible to music than their master; or the danger would have been much reduced. But the paradoxical instinct of the philosopher again reveals itself in this witty piece of irony. Of course the servants of the Danish king were not so susceptible to music as their master. Would it not, on the contrary, be very strange had it been otherwise? Do we not know that the musical sense becomes developed by exercise? That certain affections of the soul, very active in some persons, are much less so in others? That nervous sensibility is, in some degree, the heritage of the upper classes of society; and that the lower classes, whether it be on account of the manual labour to which they are subject or for any other reason, are comparatively deprived of it? It is because this inequality of organisation is both incontestable and incontested, therefore, that we have been obliged to limit, in our definition of music, the number of those upon whom it produces effect.

Nevertheless, Rousseau, though he sometimes ridiculed in this way the accounts of marvels effected by ancient music, seems to have been at other times so far inclined to believe them as to place ancient art much above modern : ancient art being one which we know very little about, but respecting which Rousseau was no better informed than ourselves. He ought to have been the last to depreciate the effects of our present music, for the enthusiasm with which he speaks of them everywhere else shows that their intensity in his own case was quite out of the common. But, however that may be, it remains a fact that, from merely ordinary observation, it would be easy to quote, in favour of the power of our music, certain facts which, to say the least, are of an authority equal to that of doubtful anecdotes by ancient historians. How often we have seen, at the performance of the *chefs d'œuvre* of our great masters, listeners agitated with dreadful spasms; crying and laughing at the same time, and manifesting all the symptoms of delirium and fever ! One young provincial musician, under the influence of passionate sentiments engendered by the "Vestale" of Spontini, could not endure the idea of returning to our prosaic world after the poetic paradise which had just been opened to him; so, after writing to inform his friends of his intention and again hearing the work which was the object of his ecstatic admiration, rightly thinking that he had attained the maximum sum of happiness reserved to man on earth, one day, at the door of the Opera he blew out his brains.

The celebrated singer, Mme. Malibran, hearing for

the first time, at the Conservatoire, the C minor Symphony of Beethoven, was seized with convulsions to such a degree that she had to be carried from the room. Twenty times have we seen, in similar cases, grave men obliged to withdraw, in order to conceal from the public the violence of their emotions. As to those which the author of this essay owes personally to music, he may at once affirm that no terms could convey an exact idea of them to those who have never made a similar experience. Without speaking of moral effects produced in him, and alluding only to impressions received and results experienced at the very moment of the execution of works which he admires, he can advance the following in all sincerity :

On hearing certain works my vital strength seems first of all doubled; I feel a delicious pleasure with which the reason has no connection; the habit of analysis then unbidden as it were to engender admiration. Emotion, increasing in direct proportion to the energy or grandeur of the composer's ideas then soon produces a strange agitation in the circulation of the blood; my arteries throb violently; tears which, in a general way, indicate the end of the paroxysm, mark in this case only a *progressive* stage which is liable to be much exceeded. In the latter case, spasmodic contractions of the muscles supervene; the limbs tremble; there is a *total numbness of the feet and hands;* a partial paralysis of the nerves of sight and hearing; in short I no longer see or hear perfectly, am seized with

giddiness and am half swooning. No doubt, sensations carried to such a degree of violence are somewhat
rare; besides which there is a vigorous contrast to be
placed against them—that of *bad musical effect* producing the contrary of admiration and pleasure. No
music acts more strongly in this direction than that
which appears to me to present the principal defects of
platitude and false expression. I then blush as if for
shame; a veritable indignation seizes me; and one
might think, to observe me, that I had just suffered
some outrage for which pardon seemed impossible. In
order to eliminate the impression thus received there is
a general rising or effort of rejection by the entire
organism, similar to the effort of vomiting when the
stomach seeks to relieve itself of some nauseous liquor.
This may be disgust and hatred carried to extreme
limits; but such music exasperates me, and I seem to
vomit it from every pore.

Of course, the habit of disguising and controlling
my feelings results in their being rarely fully displayed; and, if it has sometimes happened to me, even
since youth, to give full scope to them, this has only
arisen for want of proper time for reflection, and
because I was taken unawares.

Modern music has, accordingly, in respect of the
power which it is capable of exercising, no cause to
envy that of the ancients. At the present time let us
ask, therefore: "What are the prevalent modes of
action in musical art?" The following comprises all

those with which we are familiar; and, although they are very numerous, it is by no means proved that the future has not the discovery of some others in store.

(1) MELODY.

Musical effect produced by different sounds heard *successively;* and formed into phrases, more or less symmetrical. The art of arranging such series of different notes in an agreeable manner and of giving them an expressive signification is one which cannot be learned. It is a gift of nature; which observation of pre-existing melodies and the separate character of individuals and nations modifies in a thousand ways.

(2) HARMONY.

Musical effect produced by different sounds heard *simultaneously.* Natural dispositions can alone, no doubt, make a truly great harmonist; nevertheless, knowledge of the groups of sounds forming *chords* (generally recognised as agreeable and beautiful) as well as the art of regulating their succession, is everywhere taught with success.

(3) RHYTHM.

Symmetrical division of time by sounds. The musician cannot be *taught* to find beautiful rhythmic forms; and the particular faculty which leads to their discovery is one of the most rare. Of all elements of music that

of rhythm appears to us at the present day to be the
least advanced.

(4) EXPRESSION.

Quality by which music is brought into direct relation, in point of character, with the sentiments desired
to be rendered, or the emotions to be excited. An ac-
curate perception of this relation is far from common;
and it is not unusual to see the entire audience at the
opera, who would be disgusted at a false note, listen not
only contentedly, but even with pleasure to pieces delivered with an expression entirely false.

(5) MODULATION.

By this term we indicate, nowadays, the passage or
transition from one key, or mode, to another. Study
is capable of very greatly contributing to the musician's art in thus effectively replacing the key and
modifying its constitution appropriately. Popular
song generally modulates but slightly.

(6) INSTRUMENTATION.

This consists in allotting to each instrument what
is both suited to its peculiar nature and best calculated
to aid the effect intended to be produced. It also includes the art of so grouping the instruments as to
cause the tone of some to be modified by that of others;
and of thus causing the general effect to be of a character which no one instrument could have evolved,

even if added to others of its own class. This aspect
of instrumentation is, in music, the exact equivalent
of colour in painting. Though powerful, gorgeous and
often exaggerated at present, it was scarcely known
before the close of the eighteenth century. Precisely
as in the case of rhythm, melody and expression, we
believe that the study of models is capable of starting
the musician on the road to its full acquirement; but
that success is impossible without a special natural
disposition.

(7) Situation in Regard to the Listener.

By placing the listener at a greater or less distance
from the executants, or by separating, for certain occasions, sonorous instruments from others, we obtain
modifications of musical effect which have not yet received a due attention.

(8) Accumulation of Sound.

This is one of the most powerful principles of musical emotion. When instruments or voices are extremely
numerous and cover a great space the mass of air set
in vibration becomes enormous; and its undulations
assume a character of which, in the ordinary way, they
are deprived. This takes place to such a degree that,
in a church where there are many singers, if one of
them is heard alone, whatever may be the strength or
beauty of his voice, as exhibited in the delivery of a
theme of simple and slow character though uninter-

esting in itself, he will produce but an indifferent effect. On the other hand, let the same theme be repeated, even without much art by all the voices in unison; and it will, at once, assume an inconceivable majesty.

Of the several constituent parts of music which we have just mentioned nearly all seem to have been employed by the ancients. The only one, their possession of which is disputed, is that of *harmony*. A learned composer, our contemporary M. Lesueur, assumed, some forty years ago, the position of an intrepid antagonist of this opinion; and the views of those to whom he was opposed are set forth in the following.

They say that "*harmony was unknown to the ancients because different passages in their historians and a crowd of documents testify to the fact.* They employed nothing but the unison and octave. Moreover, it is known that harmony is an invention which does not date back further than the eighth century. The scale and tonal constitution of the ancients were not the same as ours; the latter, invented by Guido d'Arezzo, very much resembling those of plain-chant, which in its turn, is but a remnant of Greek music. It is therefore evident, for any man versed in the science of chords, that this kind of song, which does not lend itself to a harmonised accompaniment, is suited only to the unison and octave."

To this one might reply that the invention of harmony in the Middle Ages by no means proves that it was unknown in the preceding centuries. Several other items of human knowledge have been lost and rediscovered; and one of the most important which Europe attributes to itself, that of gunpowder, had been made in China long previously. It is, moreover, to say the least doubtful, with regard to the inventions of Guido d'Arezzo, whether they are really his own; for several of them are quoted by himself as universally admitted before his time. As to the difficulty of adapting plain chant to our harmony, without denying that the latter allies itself more naturally into modern melodic forms, the fact of church song being executed in counterpoint of several parts as well as accompanied by organ-chords in all churches is a sufficient reply. Let us now see upon what the opinion of M. Lesueur was based.

"Harmony was known to the ancients," he said, "because the works of their poets, philosophers and historians prove it in many places, and in peremptory fashion. These historical fragments, quite clear in themselves, have nevertheless been subject to contradictory interpretations. Thanks to the knowledge we have of Greek notation, entire pieces of their music, written for several voices, and accompanied by various instruments, are there to testify to this truth. Duets, trios and choruses of Sapho, Olympe, Terpandre, Aristoxène,* etc., faithfully reproduced by our musical

---

* Classical proper names as in the original French.

signs, will be published later on. In them, a simple and clear harmony will be discovered; consisting entirely of the most concordant combinations, and in precisely the same style as that of certain fragments of religious music composed in our own day. Both their scale and tonal system are entirely identical with our own. It is a most serious mistake to recognise in plain-chant, which is simply a monstrous tradition of barbarous hymns howled by the Druids whilst standing round the statue of Odin during the progress of horrible sacrifices, a remnant of Greek music. There are some hymns in use in the ritual of the Catholic Church which are Greek, it is true; and these we find conceived in the same system as our modern music. Moreover, even if proof by an appeal to fact should fail, would not the appeal to reason suffice to demonstrate the incorrectness of the opinion which denies to the ancients the knowledge and employment of harmony? What! the Greeks—those ingenious and polished sons of the country which gave birth to Homere, Sophocle, Pindare, Phidias, Appeles and Zeuxis*—that artistic people by whom those marvellous temples were reared which time has even yet not been able to destroy, and whose chisel carved from the marble such human forms as might worthily represent the gods—the nation whose monumental works serve as models to poets, statuaries, architects and painters

---

* Classical proper names as in the original French.

of our own day—this people possess only a kind of
music as incomplete and coarse as that of barbarians?
What! those thousands of singers of both sexes maintained at great expense in the temples, the crowd of
instruments of different nature which they mention:

"*Lyra, Psalterium, Trigonium, Sambuca, Cithara,
Pectis, Maga, Barbiton, Testudo, Epigonium, Simmi-
cium, Epandoron,* etc., as stringed instruments; and
Tuba, Fistula, Tibia, Cornu, Lituus, etc., as wind instruments; besides *Tympanum, Cymbalum, Crepitacu-
lum, Tintinnabulum, Crotalum,* etc., as instruments of
percussion; all these we are to suppose only to have
been employed to produce cold and sterile unisons or
miserable octaves! So, they must have given the same
part to both harp and trumpet—have chained together
by sheer force and for the production of a grotesque
unison two instruments the bearing, character and
effect of which are so enormously different! This is
an unmerited insult to the intelligence and musical
sense of a great people; an accusation of barbarism
against the whole of Greece."

Such was the basis of M. Lesueur's opinion. As to
the facts to which he alludes in proof, nothing can
be urged against them. If the illustrious master had
published his great work on ancient music *with* the
fragments alluded to above; if he had indicated the
sources of his information and the manuscripts which
he had brought into requisition; if the incredulous had
been enabled to convince themselves with their own

eyes that the *harmonies* attributed to the Greeks have really and visibly been bequeathed to us by them, then indeed M. Lesueur would have gained the case in advocacy of which he has worked so long with an inexhaustible perseverance and conviction. Unfortunately, he has not done so; and, as doubt is still very permissible upon this question, we shall proceed to examine the proofs of reasoning advanced by M. Lesueur; and this with the same impartiality as that brought to bear in testing the notions of his antagonists.

We shall therefore answer him as follows:

The plain chants which you call barbarous are not all so severely regarded by the generality of present-day musicians; to whom several of them appear, on the contrary, imbued with a rare character of severity and grandeur. The tonal system in which these hymns are written, and which you condemn, is susceptible of many admirable applications. Popular songs, often full of expression and simplicity, are deprived of the *leading note;* and are consequently written in the same tonal system as plain-chant; others, such as Scotch melodies, belong to a musical scale even still more strange; since both the fourth and seventh degrees of our scale are absent from it. What can be more fresh, however, or sometimes more energetic than these mountain airs? To pronounce all forms to be barbarous which are contrary to our habits is not to prove that an education different from the one we have received might not singularly modify our ideas in regard to

them. Moreover, without going so far as to tax Greece
with barbarism, we need only admit that its music, in
comparison with our own was in a state of infancy;
and to contrast the imperfect state of one art in particular with the splendour of other arts not presenting
any point of contact with it, or possessing in regard
to it any kind of relation, is not at all admissible. The
form of reasoning which seeks to pronounce this
anomaly impossible is far from new; and it is known
that, in many cases, it has led to conclusions which
the facts have subsequently disproved with a destruc-
tive ruthlessness.

The argument drawn from the musical absurdity of
allowing instruments so dissimilar in their nature as
the harp, trumpet and tympanum to go together in
the octave or unison is without any real force, for
we have only to ask whether such an instrumental disposition is practicable? Of course it is; and musicians of the present day are open to use it, whenever
they please. It is therefore not very extraordinary
that it should have been admitted by nations the very
constitution of whose art did not permit of the employment of any other.

Now, as to the superiority of our music over that of
ancient times, this certainly appears more than pro-
bable. Whether, in point of fact, the ancients understood harmony or not, by grouping together the ideas
that the partisans of the two contrary opinions have
given us of the nature and resources of their art, suffi-

cient evidence results to come to the following conclusion :

Our music includes that of the ancients; but theirs
does not include ours.   That is to say, we can easily
reproduce the effects of the music of antiquity ; and, in
addition to them, an infinite number of other effects
which they never knew; and which it was impossible
for them to render.

We have said nothing respecting Oriental music; and
for this reason.   All that we have so far gathered
from travellers respecting this subject is confined to
informal puerilities; lacking all relation to the ideas
which we attach to the term "music."   In default of
information both new and opposed on all points to
that which we have acquired, we must regard music
among the Oriental peoples as merely a grotesque
noise, analogous to that of children at play.*

---

* Since these lines were written we have had occasion, in
France and England to hear Arabian, Chinese and Persian
musicians; and every experience which it has been permitted
to us to make of their songs and their instruments, as well as
the questions we have addressed to such of them as could
speak French—all has combined to confirm us in the view expressed.   (Author's note.)

A CRITICAL STUDY OF BEETHOVEN'S
SYMPHONIES.

II.—A CRITICAL STUDY OF BEETHOVEN'S SYMPHONIES.

I T is thirty-six or thirty-seven years ago, that, at the "Concerts Spirituels" of the Opera, the trial was made of the works of Beethoven, then completely unknown in France. No one could imagine at the present day the reprobation at once heaped upon this admirable music by the majority of artists. It was strange, incoherent, diffuse; studded with crude modulations and wild harmonies, bereft of melody, of an exaggerated expression, and too noisy; besides being horribly difficult. In order to meet the conditions set down by the men of taste who then controlled the Royal Academy of Music M. Habeneck found himself obliged to make, in the very same symphonies the execution of which he organised and directed with so much care later on at the Conservatoire, monstrous cuts; such as, at the very most, might be permissible in a ballet by Gallemberg, or an opera by Gaveaux. Without these *corrections* Beethoven would not have been admitted to the honour of figuring in the programme of the "Concerts Spirituels" between a bassoon solo

and a flute concerto. At a first hearing of the passages marked with red pencil Kreutzer ran off, stopping
his ears; and it required all his courage to make up
his mind to listen to the *remaining portion* of the
Symphony in D, at other rehearsals. Let us not forget that the opinion of M. Kreutzer was, at that time,
also that of ninety-nine out of every hundred musicians in Paris; and that, without sustained effort on
the part of the insignificant fraction who held a contrary view, the greatest composer of modern times
would most likely be scarcely known to us, even yet.
The mere fact, therefore, of the execution even of fragments of Beethoven at the Opera was one of great im-
portance; to judge of which we have only to reflect
that, without it, the Society of the Conservatoire would
not have been constituted. It is to this small body
of intelligent men, and to the public, that the honour
of calling such an excellent institution into existence
must be accorded. The public—that is to say the
"real" public, in the sense of that which *does not
belong to any coterie* and which judges by sentiment
and not according to the narrow ideas and ridiculous
theories which it has formed upon the subject of art—
this public which, in spite of itself, makes mistakes,
as is proved by the fact of its frequently having to
alter its decisions, was, at the very onset, struck by
some of the eminent qualities of Beethoven. It does
not ask whether such and such a modulation bears a
due relation to some other one; whether certain har-

monics are admitted by the *magisters*; or whether *it
is permitted* to employ certain rhythms previously unknown. It simply perceives that these rhythms, these
harmonies and these modulations, set off by a noble
and passionate melody, and clothed in powerful instrumentation, make a strong impression upon it, and
in an entirely new way. Could anything further be
necessary to excite its applause? Our French public
experiences only at rare intervals the lively and ardent
emotion of which musical art is capable; but, when it
falls to its lot to become thoroughly agitated thereby,
nothing can equal its gratitude to the artist, whoever
he may be, to whom this is due. From the moment
of its first appearance, the celebrated allegretto in A
minor of the Seventh Symphony, which had been in-
serted in the Second in order to help to *pass off the
remainder*, was appreciated at its value by the public
of the "Concerts Spirituels." The pit rose in a body
with vociferous cries for its repetition; and, at a second
performance, the first movement and the scherzo of
the Symphony in D, which had not been much enjoyed
on the occasion of the first trial, met with an almost
equal success. The manifest interest which from that
time the public began to evince with regard to Beethoven doubled the strength of his defenders; and reduced, if not to silence, at least to inaction, the majority of his detractors. Thus, little by little, thanks to
those twilight rays which revealed to the far-seeing
the direction in which the sun was about to rise, the

seed developed and resulted in the foundation, almost expressly for Beethoven, of the magnificent Society of the Conservatoire, at the present day with scarcely a rival in the world.

We are about to attempt the analysis of the symphonies of this great master; beginning with the first of them, which the Conservatoire so rarely performs.

SYMPHONY NO. 1, IN C MAJOR.

SYMPHONY NO 1, IN C MAJOR.

THIS work, by its form, by its melodic style, and by its sobriety of harmony and instrumentation, is altogether distinct from the other compositions of Beethoven by which it was succeeded. The composer evidently remained in course of writing it, under the influence of Mozart's ideas; which he sometimes enlarges, and everywhere imitates with ingenuity. In the first and second parts, however, we note the occasional appearance of rhythms which are sometimes employed, it is true, by the author of "Don Giovanni"; but with great rarity, and in a much less striking fashion. The principal subject of the first allegro is a phrase of six bars; which, without presenting anything very characteristic in itself, acquires a subsequent interest by the skill with which it is treated. It is succeeded by an episodial melody in a style but slightly distinguished; when, by means of a half-cadence repeated three or four times, we arrive at an instrumental design in imitations at a fourth; our astonishment at finding which in such a place is increased by the fact that the same design has been often employed in the overtures of several French operas.

The andante contains an accompaniment for kettle-drums, *piano*, which appears nowadays as something very ordinary; but which we may nevertheless recognise as the forerunner of the startling effects which Beethoven produced later on by means of this instrument; one which had been, in general, either sparingly or badly used by his predecessors. This movement is full of charm; its theme being graceful and lending itself well to developments in fugato, by means of which the composer has been enabled to evolve both piquant and ingenious results.

The scherzo is the first-born of that family of charming humorous pieces of which Beethoven invented the form, and determined the movement; and which he substituted in nearly all his instrumental works for the minuet of Mozart and Haydn, the speed of which is but half, and the character altogether different. The one in question has an exquisite freshness, agility and grace. It is the only real novelty of the symphony; in which the poetic idea is completely absent, notwithstanding its being so grand and rich in the greater part of the works which followed. It is music admirably framed; clear, imbued with life, though but slightly accentuated; cold and sometimes mean; as for example in the final rondo—a genuine instance of musical childishness. In a word this is not Beethoven; but we are shortly to discover him.

SYMPHONY NO. 2, IN D.

SYMPHONY NO. 2, IN D.

IN this work everything is noble, energetic and stately;
the introductory largo being a *chef-d'œuvre*. The
most beautiful effects succeed one another without
confusion and always in an unexpected manner; the
song being of a touching solemnity, which, from the
very first bars imposes respect and prepares us for emotion. Already the rhythm becomes more bold, the
orchestration richer, more sonorous and varied.
Linked with this admirable adagio is an *allegro con
brio* of irresistible spirit. The *grupetto* met with in
the first bar of the opening theme, and which is given
out by violas and violoncellos in unison, is afterwards
resumed in isolated form; in order to establish either
progressions in crescendo or imitations between the
wind and string instruments, which are invariably of
a character as new as it is full of life. In the midst
of these a melody is met with, the first half of which
is given out by clarinets, horns and bassoons, but which
concludes "tutti" by the rest of the orchestra; the
virile energy of which is further enhanced by a happy

choice of accompanying chords. The andante is not treated in the same way as that of the first symphony; it is not composed of a subject worked out in canonic imitations, but of a theme pure and simple, stated in the first instance by the strings, and afterwards embroidered with rare elegance by means of light touches, the character of which is always strictly in keeping with the sentiment of tenderness which forms the distinctive trait of the principal idea. It is the delineation of innocent happiness hardly clouded by a few accents of melancholy occurring at rare intervals.

The scherzo is just as frankly gay in its capricious fantasy as the andante was completely happy and calm; for everything in this symphony is genial, even the warlike sallies of the first allegro being exempt from violence, so that one can trace in them no more than the youthful ardour of a noble heart which retains intact the most beautiful illusions of life. The composer still has faith in immortal glory, in love and self-sacrifice. Hence the degree to which he abandons himself to his gaiety, and the felicity of his sallies of wit. To hear the different instruments disputing the possession of some portion of a motive, which no one of them executes entirely, but of which each fragment becomes in this way coloured with a thousand different tints in passing from one to the other, one might easily indulge the fancy of being present at the fairy gambols of the graceful spirits of Oberon. The finale is of the same nature; it is a second scherzo in duple measure; the playfulness of which is perhaps, to some extent, even more refined and piquant.

SYMPHONY NO. 3, IN E FLAT.

(THE "EROICA.")

C

SYMPHONY NO. 3, IN E FLAT.
(THE "EROICA.")

I T is extremely wrong to tamper with the description placed at the head of this work by the composer himself. The inscription runs: "Heroic Symphony to celebrate the memory of a great man." In this we see that there is no question of battles or triumphal marches such as many people, deceived by mutilations of the title naturally expect; but much in the way of grave and profound thought, of melancholy souvenirs and of ceremonies imposing by their grandeur and sadness—in a word, it is the hero's *funeral rites.* I know few examples in music of a style in which grief has been so consistently able to retain such pure form and such nobleness of expression.

The first movement is in triple time and at a degree of speed nearly equal to that of the waltz. But, nevertheless, what can be more serious or more dramatic than this allegro? The energetic theme which forms its foundation does not at first present itself in its entirety. Contrary to custom the composer, in commencing, has only allowed us a glimpse of his melodic idea; it does not present itself in its full effect until after an exordium of some bars. The rhythm is particularly remarkable by the frequency of syncopation and by combinations of duple measure; thrown, by accentuation of the weak beat, into the triple bar. When, with this disjointed rhythm, rude dissonances come to present themselves in combination, like those we find near the middle of the second repeat, where the first violins strike F natural against E (the fifth in the chord of A minor) it is impossible to repress a sensation of fear at such a picture of ungovernable fury. It is the voice of despair, almost of rage.

Still, it may be asked—why this despair? Why this rage? The motive of it does not appear The orchestra becomes calm at the following bar; as if, exhausted by the excess to which it had given way, its strength began suddenly to fail. Moreover, the phrases are now gentle; and we find in them all that remembrance is capable of suggesting to the soul of the nature of sad regrets. It is impossible to describe or even to indicate, the multitude of melodic and harmonic aspects in which Beethoven reproduces his theme; we will confine ourselves to the mention of one which is extremely strange, which has formed the text of many discussions, and which the French editor corrected in the score, imagining it to be a mistake of the engraver; but which was, later on, re-instated—as the result of more ample information.

The first and second violins alone hold, in tremolo,

the major second B flat, A flat (part of the chord of the dominant seventh in E flat); when a horn, having quite the appearance of being at fault and of coming in four bars too soon, starts timidly with the commencement of the principal theme; running exclusively on the notes—E flat, G, E flat, B flat. One may imagine the strange effect produced by this melody, formed of the three notes of the tonic chord, against the two dissonant notes of the chord of the dominant; notwithstanding the harshness being much reduced by separation of the parts. But, at the moment when the ear is inclined to revolt against such an anomaly, a vigorous tutti interrupts the horn; and, concluding *piano* on the tonic chord, allows the violoncellos to return; who then state the entire theme with its natural harmony. Looking at things broadly it is difficult to find a serious justification for this musical caprice.* They say, however, that the composer was very strenuous upon the point; and it is even related that, at the first rehearsal of this symphony, M. Ries being present stopped the orchestra by calling out—"Too soon! too soon!—The horn is wrong!" and that the only reward for his zeal was that he received from Beethoven, who was furious, a sharp lecture.

---

* Whichever way we look at it, if the above is really an intention of Beethoven, and if there is any truth in the anecdotes which are current upon the subject, it must be admitted to be a whim amounting to absurdity. (Author's note.)

No other eccentricity of this nature is to be found in the rest of the score; and the Funeral March is a drama in itself. We seem to trace in it the translation of those beautiful lines of Virgil on the funeral procession of the young Pallas—

> Multa que præterea Laurentis præmia pugnæ
> Adgerat, et longo prædam jubet ordine duci.
> Post bellator equus, positis insignibus, Æthon
> It lacrymans, guttis que humectat grandibus ora.

The end, especially, is profoundly moving. The march-theme reappears; but in fragments, interspersed by silence, and without any other accompaniment than three notes *pizzicato* by the double bass. When these shreds of the lugubrious melody thus alone, bare, broken and effaced, have one by one passed on to the tonic, the wind instruments raise a cry which is the last adieu of the warriors to their companion in arms; and the entire orchestra dies away on an organ-point, *pianissimo.*

The third movement is entitled Scherzo, according to custom. In Italian the word signifies "play," or "humorous frolic." At first sight it does not appear obvious how such a style of music can figure in an epic composition. To realise this it must be heard. The rhythm and the movement of the scherzo are, indeed, there. There is also play; but it is play of funereal kind, at every instant clouded by thoughts of mourning—a kind of play, in fact, recalling that which the warriors of the Iliad celebrated round the tombs of their chiefs.

Even in the most capricious evolutions of his orchestra Beethoven knew how to preserve the grave and sombre tint, as well as the profound sadness which ought naturally to dominate in such a case. The *finale* is nothing but a development of the same poetic idea. One very curious passage of instrumentation is to be remarked at the commencement; showing what effect can be drawn from the opposition of different *timbres*. It is a B flat taken by the violins, and repeated immediately by the flutes and oboes; in the style of an echo. Although the repercussion takes place on the same note of the scale, at the same movement and with equal force, so great a difference results from this dialogue that the nuance which distinguishes the instruments from one another might be compared to that between *blue* and *violet*. Such refinements of tone-colour were altogether unknown before Beethoven; and it is to him that we owe them.

The finale, though so varied, consists entirely of a very simple *fugato* theme; upon which the composer afterwards builds, in addition to numerous ingenious details, two other themes; one of the latter being of extreme beauty. The outline of this melody does not enable one to perceive that it has, so to speak, been extracted from another one. Its expression, on the contrary, is much more touching; and it is incomparably more graceful than the first theme, the character of which is rather that of a bass—a function which it fulfils extremely well. This melody reappears shortly before the close, in a slower degree of movement, and with new harmonies, by which the effect of its sadness is increased. The hero causes many tears; but, after the last regrets paid to his memory, the poet turns aside from elegy; in order to intone with transport his hymn of glory. It may be somewhat laconic, but this peroration rises to a high effect and worthily crowns the musical monument. Beethoven has written works more striking perhaps that this symphony; and several of his other compositions impress the public in a more lively way. But it must be allowed, notwithstanding, that the "Sinfonia Eroica" possesses such strength of thought and execution, that its style is so emotional and consistently elevated besides its form being so poetical, that it is entitled to rank as equal to the highest conceptions of its composer.

A sentiment of sadness not only grave but, so to speak, antique takes possession of me whenever I hear this symphony although the public seem indifferently touched by it. We must certainly deplore the misfortune of an artist who, consumed by such enthusiasm, fails to make himself sufficiently well understood, even by a refined audience, to ensure the raising of his hearers up to the level of his own inspiration. It is all the more sad as the same audience, on other occasions, becomes ardent, excited or sorrowful along with him. It becomes seized with a real and lively passion for some of his compositions; equally admirable, it may be admitted, but nevertheless not more beautiful than the present work. It appreciates at their just value the allegretto in A minor of the seventh symphony; the allegretto scherzando of the eighth; the finale of the fifth and the scherzo of the ninth. It even appears to experience emotion at the funeral march of the symphony of which we are now speaking (the "Eroica"); but, in respect of the first movement, it is impossible to indulge in any illusion; for twenty years of observation tend to assure me that the public listen to it with a feeling approaching coldness, and appear to recognise in it a learned and energetic composition, but nothing beyond that. No philosophy is applicable to this case; for it is useless to say that it has always been so, and that everywhere the same fate has befallen all high productions of the human mind. Also, that the causes of poetic emotion are secret and inappreciable, that the conception of certain beauties with which particular individuals are gifted is absolutely lacking in the multitude, or that it is even impossible that it should be otherwise. All that is of no consolation. It does not calm the indignation with which one's heart is filled—an indignation instinctive, involuntary, and, it may even be, absurd—at the aspect of a marvel which is misunderstood; of a composition so noble which is regarded by the crowd without being perceived; listened to without being understood; and allowed to pass by without courting any attention;

precisely as if it were a mere case of something medi-
ocre or indifferent.   Oh! it is frightful to be obliged
to acknowledge with a pitiless conviction that what I
find beautiful may constitute *beauty* for me, but that it
may not do so for my best friend; that he, whose sympathy generally corresponds with my own, may be
affected in a totally different way; and that even the
work which affords me a transport of pleasure—which
excites me to the utmost, and which moves me to tears,
may leave him cold; and may even cause him dis-
pleasure and annoyance.

The majority of great poets have little feeling for
music, and enjoy only trivial and childish melodies.
Many highly intellectual people who think they love
it have little idea of the emotion it is able to raise.
These are sad truths; but they are so palpable and
evident that nothing but the illusion caused by certain
systems can stand in the way of their recognition.   I
have observed a dog bark with pleasure on hearing a
major third, executed *sostenuto* by double-stopping
upon the violin; but the offspring of the same animal
were not in the least affected, either by the third, fifth,
sixth or octave—or, in fact, by any chord whatever.
whether consonant or dissonant.   The public, however
it may be composed, is always, in respect of great
musical conceptions, in a similar position.   It has
certain nerves which vibrate in sympathy with certain
forms of resonance.   But this organisation, incomplete
as it is, is unequally distributed; as well as subject to

no end of modifications. It follows that it would be almost foolish to count upon such and such artistic means in preference to others for the purpose of acting upon it. Thus the composer is best advised to follow blindly his own individual sentiment; resigning himself beforehand to the results which chance may have in store.

One day I was coming out of the conservatoire with three or four amateurs; the occasion being a performance of the "Choral" Symphony.

"What do you think of that work?" said one of them to me.

"Immense! Magnificent! Overpowering!"

"That is singular. For my part, I found it cruelly tiresome. And you?" added the speaker addressing an Italian.

"Oh! as for me, I find it obscure; or rather unpleasant, for there is no melody."

But, besides that, note the different views which several journals express about it:

"The Choral Symphony of Beethoven represents the culminating point of modern music. Art has hitherto produced nothing to be compared with it in respect of nobleness of style, grandeur of plan and refinement of detail."

(Another journal)—"The Choral Symphony of Beethoven is a monstrosity."

(Another)—"This work is not altogether lacking in

ideas; but they are badly disposed and the general effect is incoherent and devoid of charm."

(Another)—"The Choral Symphony of Beethoven contains some admirable passages; though it is evident that the composer lacked ideas and that, his exhausted imagination no longer sustaining him, he made considerable effort, and often with some success, in order to replace inspiration by artistic resources. The few phrases which we meet with in it are handled in a superior manner and disposed in a perfectly clear and logical order. On the whole, it is the highly interesting work of a *used-up* genius."

Where shall we find the truth or where the error? Everywhere, and yet in no particular place. Each one is right; for what is beautiful for one is not so for another. This naturally follows, if only from the fact that one has experienced emotion whilst the other has remained unaffected; that the first has received a lively enjoyment, whilst the second has suffered an intense fatigue. What can be done in such a case? Nothing. But it is distressing, and makes me feel inclined to prefer the foolish view of beauty being absolute.

SYMPHONY NO. 4, IN B FLAT.

SYMPHONY NO. 4, IN B FLAT.

H ERE Beethoven entirely abandons ode and elegy; in order to return to the less elevated and less sombre, but not less difficult style of the second symphony. The general character of this score is either lively, alert and gay or of a celestial sweetness. With the exception of the meditative adagio, which serves as its introduction, the first movement is almost entirely given over to joy. The motive in detached notes, with which the allegro opens, is only a background upon which the composer is afterwards enabled to display other melodies of more real character; the effect of the latter being to impart a secondary character to what was apparently the principal idea of the commencement.

This artifice, although fertile in curious and interesting results, had already been employed by Mozart and Haydn with equal success. But we find in the second part of the same allegro, a really new idea, the first few bars of which arrest attention; and which also, after interesting the listener by its mysterious

developments, strikes him with astonishment by its unexpected conclusion.   It is composed as follows:

After a fairly vigorous *tutti* the first violins parcel
out the original theme, by forming a dialogue in
pianissimo with their seconds.   This terminates with
holding notes of the dominant chord of the key of B
natural; each instance of such holding notes being
followed by two bars of silence interrupted only by a
light *tremolo* of the kettledrum; which, being tuned to
B flat, plays enharmonically the part of third to the
fundamental F sharp.   After two such appearances the
kettledrum ceases; in order to allow the string instruments an opportunity of sweetly murmuring other
fragments of the theme, and of arriving by a new enharmonic modulation to the chord of six-four; second
inversion of that of B flat.   The kettledrum now
returns upon the same sound; which, instead of being
a leading note, as upon the first occasion, is now a
veritable tonic; and, as such, continues the *tremolo* for
some twenty bars.   The force of tonality possessed by
this B flat, only slightly perceptible at first, becomes
greater in the same degree as the *tremolo* proceeds.
Afterwards, the other instruments, bestrewing the
onward march with slight and unfinished traits, pre-
pare us for a continuous roll of the kettledrum on a
general *forte*, in which the perfect chord of B flat is
finally stated by the full orchestra in all its majesty.
This remarkable *crescendo* is one of the best conceived
effects which we know of in all music; and its counter-

part can scarcely be found elsewhere than in the similar feature by which the celebrated scherzo of the C
minor Symphony is concluded. The latter, however,
notwithstanding its immense effect, is conceived upon
a scale less vast, starting from *piano* in order to arrive
at the final explosion, without departing from the original key. On the other hand, the episode we are now
describing starts from *mezzo forte;* and is afterwards
lost for a moment in a *pianissimo*, whilst harmonised
in a manner constantly vague and undecided. Then,
it reappears with chords of a somewhat more settled
tonality; and bursts forth only at the moment when
the cloud which enshrouded the modulation has completely disappeared. It might be compared to a river,
the peaceful waters of which suddenly disappear and
only emerge from their subterranean bed to form a
furious and foaming waterfall.

As for the adagio, it seems to elude analysis. Its
form is so pure and the expression of its melody so
angelic and of such irresistible tenderness that the
prodigious art by which this perfection is attained disappears completely. From the very first bars we are
overtaken by an emotion which, towards the close,
becomes so overpowering in its intensity that only
amongst the giants of poetic art can we find anything
to compare with this sublime page of the giant of
music. Nothing in fact more resembles the impression
produced by this adagio than that experienced when
reading the touching episode of Francesca di Rimini

in the "Divina Comedia"; the recital of which Virgil
could not hear without sobbing bitterly; and which,
at the last line, causes Dante to fall *like a dead body*.
This movement seems as if it had been sadly mur-
mured by the Archangel Michael on some day when,
overcome by a feeling of melancholy, he contemplated
the universe from the threshold of the Empyrean.

The scherzo consists almost exclusively of phrases
in duple rhythm, forcibly forming part of combinations in triple time. This means, which Beethoven
uses frequently, imparts verve to the style; the melodic
outlines become sharper and more surprising, besides
which these rhythms, running counter to the ordinary
beat, present an independent charm which is very real,
although difficult to explain. A pleasure results from
this disturbance of the normal accent, which regains
its position at the end of each period; the sense of the
musical discourse, which had been for a time suspended, then arriving at a satisfactory conclusion and
complete solution.

The melody of the trio, confided to the wind instruments, is of a delicious freshness; its movement being
slower than that of the rest of the scherzo, and its elegant simplicity being enhanced by encountering the
opposition of short phrases emanating from the violins, which seem cast upon the surface of the harmony
like charming traits of innocent mischief. The finale,
which is both gay and sprightly, returns to ordinary
rhythmic forms. It is one animated swarm of spark-

ling notes, presenting a continual babble; interrupted,
however, by occasional rough and uncouth chords, in
which the angry interspersions, which we have already
had occasion to mention as peculiar to this composer,
are again manifest.

SYMPHONY NO. 5, IN C MINOR.

SYMPHONY NO. 5, IN C MINOR.

THE most celebrated of all is also, without question, in our opinion, the one in which Beethoven gives free scope to his vast imagination; without electing to be either guided or supported by any outside thought. In the first, second and fourth symphonies he more or less extended forms which were already known; investing them with the poetry of a brilliant and passionate inspiration due to his vigorous youth. In the third (the "Eroica") the form tends to a greater breadth, it is true; the thought also reaching to a greater height. Notwithstanding all this, however, we cannot fail to recognise therein the influence of one or other of those divine poets to whom, for so long, the great artist had erected a temple in his heart. Beethoven, faithful to the precept of Horace:

Nocturnâ versate manu, versate diurnâ,

used to read Homer habitually; and, in his magnificent musical epic which, rightly or wrongly, is said to have been inspired by a modern hero, remembrances of the antique "Iliad" play an admirable and beautiful, but no less evident part.

The Symphony in C minor, on the other hand, appears to us to emanate directly and solely from the genius of Beethoven. It is his own intimate thought which is there developed; and his secret sorrows, his pent-up rage, his dreams so full of melancholy oppression, his nocturnal visions and his bursts of enthusiasm furnish its entire subject; whilst the melodic, harmonic, rhythmic and orchestral forms are there delineated with an essential novelty and individuality, endowing .them also with considerable power and nobleness.

The first movement is devoted to the expression of the disordered sentiments which pervade a great soul when a prey to despair. It is not that calm and concentrated despair which bears the outward appearance of resignation; or the grief, so sombre and silent, which Romeo evinces on hearing of the death of Juliet. Rather is it the terrible fury of Othello, when receiving from the mouth of Iago the empoisoned calumnies which persuade him of Desdemona's crime. Sometimes it is a frenzied delirium, bursting forth in fearful cries. Sometimes it is an excessive depression, expressing itself only in accents of regret and seeming to hold itself in pity. Listen to those orchestral gasps; to those chords in dialogue between wind and strings, which come and go whilst gradually growing weaker, like the painful respiration of a dying man. These at last give place to a phrase full of violence;

in which the orchestra seems to rise again reanimated by a spark of fury. See that quivering mass; which hesitates for an instant, and then precipitates itself, bodily divided, into two ardent unisons, resembling two streams of lava. And then, having done this, say whether this passionate style is not both beyond and above anything which had been yet produced in instrumental music.

This movement presents a striking example of the effect produced by the excessive doubling of parts under certain circumstances, and of the wild aspect of the chord of the fourth on the second note of the scale; otherwise described as the second inversion of the chord of the dominant. It is met with frequently without either preparation or resolution, and it even occurs once without the leading note and on an organ point; the D forming the bass of the strings, whilst the G forms the discordant summit of a few parts assigned to the wind.

The adagio presents some characteristic relation with the allegretto in A minor of the Seventh Symphony; and with that in E flat of the fourth. It offers equally the melancholy gravity of the first and the touching grace of the second. The theme, first stated by the violoncellos and violas, together with a simple pizzicato double-bass accompaniment, is followed by a certain phrase for wind instruments which recurs continually in the same form and in the same key from one end to the other of the movement, whatever may be the successive modifications to which the original theme is subject. This persistence of one and the same phrase, in adhering always to its original simplicity, is so profoundly sad that it produces, little by little, upon the soul of the listener an impression impossible to describe, but which is certainly the most powerful of its kind which we have ever experienced.

Among the boldest harmonic effects of this sublime elegy may be quoted :

(1). The sostenuto of an upper part on the dominant B flat whilst the strings move rapidly below; passing by the chord of the sixth (D flat, F, B flat), to which the said upper part does not belong.

(2). The incidental phrase executed by flute, oboe and two clarinets, proceeding in contrary motion and giving rise, from time to time, to unprepared discords of the second between G, the leading note, and F, as major sixth in the key of A flat. This third inversion of the chord of the seventh on the leading note is forbidden by most theorists, precisely as the upper pedal just mentioned; though it does not, on that account, present any less delightful effect. There is also, at the last entry of the original theme, a *canon in the unison at one bar distance* between violins and flutes, clarinets and bassoons. This would give to the melody thus treated a new interest, were it possible to hear the imitation of the wind instruments; but, unfortunately, just then the entire orchestra is playing so loud as to render it inaudible.

The scherzo is a strange composition, the first bars of which, though presenting nothing terrible, cause that strange emotion we are accustomed to experience under the magnetic glance of certain individuals. Everything in it is mysterious and sombre; the orchestral devices, with more or less sinister aspect, seeming to belong to the same order of ideas which created the famous Eloksberg scene in Goethe's "Faust." Tints of *piano* and *mezzo-forte* prevail throughout. The middle part, or trio, is remarkable for a bass passage executed with all the force of the bow; the uncouth weight of which shakes the very feet of the players' desks and resembles somewhat the gambols of a delighted elephant. But the monster departs, and the noise of his mad careering gradually dies away. The motive of the scherzo now reappears in *pizzicato;* peace is gradually regained; until nothing more is heard than a few notes, daintily plucked by the violins, and the faintly strange clucking produced by the bassoons, giving their high A flat, closely opposed by G, as octave in the chord of the dominant minor ninth. Then, interrupting the cadence, the stringed instruments *col arco* softly take the chord of A flat, upon which they repose for a length of time. The rhythm is entirely dependent upon the kettledrums, by which it is sustained in the form of light strokes given by sponge-covered sticks; its design thus appearing in dull form against the general stagnation of the rest of the orchestra.

The kettledrum note is C, and the key of the movement that of C minor; but the chord of A flat, long
sustained by the other instruments, seems, on the one
hand, to introduce a different tonality, whilst, on the
other, the isolated *martellato* of the kettledrum on C
tends to preserve the sentiment of the original key.
The ear hesitates, uncertain as to the way in which this
harmonic mystery is about to issue; when the dull
pulsations of the kettledrum, becoming more and more
intense, meet the violins who have now rejoined the
rhythmic movement and changed the harmony. The
chord is now that of the dominant seventh (G, B, D, F),
throughout which the kettledrums obstinately continue
their roll upon C tonic. And then it is that the entire
orchestra, reinforced by the trombones which have
hitherto not appeared, bursts forth in the major mode
upon a triumphal march-theme, and the finale begins.
Everybody knows the effect of this thunder stroke;
and it is, therefore, useless to detain the reader with
any account of it.

The critics have nevertheless tried to detract from
the merit of the composer by declaring that, in the
above, he had resorted to a mere vulgar procedure;
the brightness of the major mode pompously succeeding the obscurity of the minor *pianissimo*. Also, that
the triumphal theme was lacking in originality, and
that the interest grew less as the end was approached,
instead of following a contrary order.

To this we may reply by asking :

Was less genius necessary to create such a work because the passage from *piano* to *forte* and that from *minor* to *major* were means already known?

How many other composers have resorted to the same means, and how far can the results which they have obtained be compared to this gigantic song of victory; in which the soul of the poet-musician, henceforth free from all hindrance and earthly suffering, seems to rise beaming towards the very heavens? The first four bars of the theme are, it is true, not of great originality; but the forms of the fanfare are naturally restricted; and we do not believe it would be possible to discover new ones without altogether emerging from the simple, grand and pompous character which is proper to it. Beethoven, therefore, required only a fanfare entrance for his finale; and, throughout the rest of the movement, and even in the part succeeding the principal phrase, he retains the elevation and novelty of style which never abandons him. As to the reproach of not having proceeded with an increasing interest to the conclusion the following may be replied :

Music cannot, at all events in the state in which we know it, produce a more violent effect than that of the transition from the scherzo to the triumphal march. It was, therefore, quite impossible to proceed with any augmentation of it.

To *sustain* such a height of effect is, in fact, already a prodigious effort. Notwithstanding the amplitude of the developments in which Beethoven has indulged, he has succeeded in accomplishing this. But this very equality between the commencement and conclusion suffices to cause a *suspicion* of decrease, on account of the terrible shock which the nerves of the listener experience at the opening. Nervous emotion, thus raised to its most violent paroxysm, becomes immediately afterwards so much the more difficult to effect. In a long row of columns of similar height an optical illusion causes those which are most removed to appear smaller than the rest. Possibly our feeble organisation would be better suited to a laconic peroration such as :

Notre général vous rappelle,

by Gluck. The audience would, in this way, not have time to grow cold; and the symphony would finish before fatigue had intervened to prevent the possibility of accompanying the author in his advance. This observation, however, only applies, so to speak, to the *mise-en-scène* of the work; and by no means prevents this finale from being in itself of a magnificence and richness in comparison with which there are few pieces which could appear without being completely crushed.

SYMPHONY NO. 6, IN F.

(THE "PASTORAL.")

SYMPHONY NO. 6, IN F
(THE "PASTORAL.")

THIS astonishing landscape seems as if it were the joint work of Poussin and Michael Angelo. A desire to depict the calm of the country-side and the shepherd's gentle ways now actuates the composer of "Fidelio" and of the "Eroïca." But let us understand one another; for here is no question of the gaily bedecked shepherds of M. de Florian, and still less of those of M. Lebrun, author of "Rossignol," or of those of J.-J. Rousseau, author of the "Devin de Village." The question is of Nature, in all its simple truth.

The composer entitles his first movement:

"Erwachen heiterer Empfindungen bei der Aukunft auf dem Lande."*

The herdsmen begin to appear in the fields. They have their usual careless manner, and the sound of

---

* Berlioz's rendering of this original title is—"Sensations douces qu'inspire l'aspect d'un riant pay sage"; or—"The awakening of cheerful feelings at first aspect of the country.' (Translator s note.)

their pipes proceeds from far and near. Delightful
phrases greet you, like the perfumed morning breeze;
and swarms of chattering birds in flight pass rustling
overhead. From time to time the atmosphere seems
charged with vapour; great clouds appear and hide the
sun; then, all at once, they disappear; and there suddenly falls upon both tree and wood the torrent of a
dazzling light. That is the effect, as it appears to me,
on hearing this movement; and I believe that, notwithstanding the vagueness of instrumental expression,
many listeners have been impressed by it in the same way.

Farther on, there is the "Scene am Bach";* devoted
to contemplation. No doubt the author created this
admirable adagio whilst reclining on the grass; gazing
upwards, listening to the wind, and fascinated by the
surrounding soft reflections of both light and sound;
at one and the same time looking at, and listening to,
the tiny white waves as they sparkled along; and, with
a slight murmur, broke upon the pebbles of the brink.
It is indeed beautiful.

There are some persons who strongly reproach Beethoven with having, at the end of the adagio, endeav-
oured to reproduce the song of three birds. As, in my
opinion, it is success or non-success which decides about
the absurdity or otherwise of such attempts, I may tell

---

* Berlioz's translation of this original title is: "Scène au
bord de la rivière"—or, "Scene at the brook." (Translator's
note.)

the adverse critics in this instance that their stricture appears justifiable, so far as the nightingale is concerned; as the song of this bird is scarcely better imitated here than in the famous flute solo of M. Lebrun; for the simple reason that the nightingale emits only sounds which are inappreciable and variable, and which cannot, therefore, be rendered by instruments with fixed tones playing in a certain key. It seems to me, however, that this does not apply either to the quail or to the cuckoo; the respective cries of which are—two notes in one case, and one in the other—notes true and determined, and admitting therefore of an imitation exact and complete.

Now, if the musician is to be accused of puerility because he renders exactly the song of birds in a scene where all the calm voices alike of heaven, earth and waterfall find naturally their place, I may answer that the same objection could also be addressed to him when, in a storm, he applies a similar treatment to the winds, the claps of thunder, or the bellowing of cattle. Providence, however, can only tell whether it has ever entered the head of one of these critics to blame the *storm of the "Pastoral" Symphony!*

But let us continue. The poet now leads us into the midst of a

"Lustiges Zusammensein der Landleute."*

---

* Berlioz's rendering of this original title is: "Réunion joyeuse de paysans," or: "Joyous meeting of country folk." (Translator's note.)

They laugh and dance with moderation at first; whilst, from the Musette, there issues a gay refrain, accompanied by a bassoon, which seems only able to intone two notes. Beethoven has probably intended this to represent some good old German peasant, mounted on a barrel and armed with a dilapidated instrument, from which he just succeeds in drawing the two principal notes of the key of F; its tonic and dominant. Every time the oboe gives out its musette-like melody, which seems as simple and gay as a young girl dressed out in her Sunday clothes, the old bassoon brings out his two notes. Should the melodic phrase modulate at all, the bassoon is silent; quietly counting his rests until the return of the principal key permits him to come in again with his imperturbable—"F, C, F." This effect, so excellently grotesque, seems almost completely to escape the attention of the public.

The dance now becomes more animated, excited and noisy. The rhythm changes, and a melody of grosser character in duple time announces the arrival of the mountaineers with their heavy *sabots*. The portion in triple time now recommences more animatedly than ever. The whole becomes confused, and gathers force; flowing locks begin to fall upon the shoulders of the peasant-women; the mountaineers have brought with them a wine-inspired and demonstrative joy; there is clapping of hands, they cry, they run and precipitate themselves—in short, there is a climax of excitement.

But, all at once, there comes the distant thunder,
spreading fear throughout the company of this *bal
champêtre* and putting all the dancers to flight.

"Gewitter—Sturm.' *

I despair of being able to give an idea of this prodigious movement. It must be heard in order to form
an idea of the degree of truth and sublimity descriptive music can attain in the hands of a man like Beethoven. Listen!—listen to those rain-charged squalls
of wind; to the dull grumblings of the basses; also to
the keen whistling of the piccolo, which announces to
us that a horrible tempest is on the point of breaking
out. The hurricane approaches and grows in force; an
immense chromatic feature, starting from the heights
of the instrumentation, pursues its course until it gropes
its way to the lowest orchestral depths. There it
secures the basses, dragging them with it upwards; the
whole shuddering like a whirlwind sweeping everything before it. Then, the trombones burst forth, the
thunder of the kettledrums becomes redoubled in violence, it is no longer merely rain and wind, but an
awful cataclysm, the universal deluge—the end of the
world. This literally produces giddiness; and many
people, when they hear this storm, can scarcely tell
whether their emotion is one of pleasure or of pain.

---

* Berlioz's rendering is: "*Orage, éclairs*"; or: "Storm,
thunder and lightning." (Translator's note.)

The symphony concludes with :

"Hirtengesang.
Frohe, dankbare Gefühle nach dem Sturm.' *

when everything resumes its cheerfulness. The herdsmen reappear upon the mountains, calling together
their scattered flocks; the sky is serene, the rain has
almost disappeared and calm returns. With its re-
appearance we hear again those rustic songs the gentle
melody of which is such repose to the soul after the
consternation and shock produced by the magnificent
horror of the previous picture.

After that, can anyone really consider it necessary
to allude to any strangeness of style which may be
met with in this gigantic work? Shall we take exception to the five-note groups of violoncellos, opposed to
those of four notes in the double basses, which jostle
one another without ever subsiding into unison? Must
we exclaim about the horn-call, which arpeggios the
chord of C whilst the stringed instruments are holding
that of F ?

Truly, I cannot do it. For a task of this nature one
must reason coldly; and how can we be guaranteed
from excitement when the mind is preoccupied with
such a subject! Far from that, one would like to go
to sleep for entire months, so as to dwell in imagina

---

* Berlioz's rendering is : "L'action de grâces des paysans
après le retour du beau temps"; or; "Song of the peasants;
their happy thankful feeling after the storm."

tion in that unknown sphere of which genius has given us for a moment a glimpse. If, unfortunately, one were obliged, after such a concert, to attend either a comic opera or a soirée of fashionable songs or flute concertos, the effect would be to make one feel quite stupid; so that, to the inquiry:

"How did you like that Italian duet?"

One might gravely answer:

"Very fine."

"And those clarinet variations?"

"Superb."

"And the finale of the new opera?"

"Admirable."

Any distinguished artist who might happen to hear these answers without knowing the cause of your pre-occupation would be sure to think:

Whoever is that madman?

*   *   *   *   *   *

How the antique poems, however beautiful or admired they may be, pale into insignificance when compared with this marvel of modern music! Theocritus and Virgil were great in singing the praises of landscape beauty, and the following lines present a sweet music:

Tu quoque, magna Pales, et te memorande, canemus
Pastor ab amphryso; vos Sylvæ amnes que Lycæi,

especially if they are not recited by barbarians like

Frenchmen, who pronounce Latin in such a way as to cause it to be mistaken for the patois of Auvergne.

But this poem of Beethoven!—these long periods so richly coloured!—these living pictures!—these perfumes!—that light!—that eloquent silence!—that vast horizon!—those enchanted nooks secreted in the woods!—those golden harvests!—those rose-tinted clouds like wandering flecks upon the surface of the sky!—that immense plain seeming to slumber beneath the rays of the mid-day sun!—Man is absent, and Nature alone reveals itself to admiration!—and this profound repose of everything that lives! This happy life of all which is at rest!—the little brook which runs rippling towards the river!—the river itself, parent of waters, which, in majestic silence, flows down to the great sea!—Then, Man intervenes; he of the fields, robust and God-fearing—his joyous diversion is interrupted by the storm—and we have his terror, his hymn of gratitude.

Veil your faces! ye poor, great, ancient poets—poor Immortals! Your conventional diction with all its harmonious purity can never engage in contest with the art of sounds. You are glorious, but vanquished! You never knew what we now call melody; harmony; the association of different qualities of tone; instrumental colouring; modulation; the learned conflict of discordant sounds, which first engage in combat, only afterwards to embrace; our musical surprises; and those strange accents which set in vibration the most unexplored depths of the human soul. The stammerings of the childlike art which you named Music could give you no idea of this. You alone were the great melodists and harmonists—the masters of rhythm and expression for the cultivated spirits of your time.

But these words bore, in all your tongues, a meaning quite different from that which is nowadays their due. The art of sounds, properly so-called and independent of everything, is a birth of yesterday. It is scarcely yet of age, with its adolescence. It is all powerful; it is the Pythian Apollo of the moderns. We are indebted to it for a whole world of feelings and sensations from which you were entirely shut out.

Yes! great and adored poets! you are conquered :

Inclyte sed victi.

SYMPHONY NO. 7, IN A.

SYMPHONY NO. 7, IN A.

THE seventh symphony is celebrated for its alle-gretto.* This does not arise because the other three parts are any less worthy of admiration; far from it. But the public does not generally judge by any other measure than that of effect produced; and, as it only measures this effect by the amount of applause, it follows that whatever is most applauded always passes for being the most beautiful, notwithstanding that there are beauties of infinite worth which are not of a nature to excite any demonstrations of approval. Then it happens that, in order to promote still further the object of this predilection, all the rest is sacrificed to it. Such is, at all events in France, the universal custom. That is why, in speaking of Beethoven, one says: the "storm" of the "Pastoral" Symphony; the "finale" of the Symphony in C minor; the "andante" of the Symphony in A, and so on.

It does not appear to be certain that the latter was

---

* Which they always call either adagio or andante. (Author's note.)

composed after the "Pastoral" or "Eroïca" Symphonies. Several authorities hold, on the contrary,
that it preceded these symphonies by a certain period
of time. The mere number which designates it as the
seventh would, consequently, should this opinion be
well-founded, refer merely to the order of publication.

The first movement opens with a broad and pompous
introduction, in which melody, modulations and orchestral designs successively compete for the hearer's interest; besides commencing with one of those effects of
instrumentation of which Beethoven is incontestibly
the creator. The entire mass, striking a chord both
loud and short, discovers an oboe during the silence
which succeeds. The entrance of this oboe, hidden by
the orchestral attack, had not been previously perceived; and it now states the opening melody in *sostenuto*. No more original mode of opening could be
imagined. At the end of the introduction the note E
(as dominant of A), recalled after several excursions
into neighbouring keys, becomes the object of a play
of tone-colour between violins and flutes somewhat
analogous to that met with in the first few bars of the
finale of the "Eroïca" Symphony. This E comes and
goes without accompaniment during six bars; changing its aspect each time it passes from string to wind.
Finally, retained by flute and oboe, it serves to join
the introduction to the allegro; and becomes the first
note of the principal theme, of which it gradually outlines the rhythmical form. I have heard this subject

ridiculed on account of its rustic simplicity. Probably the reproach of lack of nobleness would never
have been applied to it had the author, as in the "Pastoral" Symphony, placed at the head of his allegro in
plain letters the inscription :

"Ronde de Paysans"; (Peasants' Rondo).

We therefore see that, if there are listeners who
prefer *not* to be warned of the subject treated by the
musician, there are others, on the contrary, indisposed
to welcome any idea presented to them in an unaccus-
tomed dress, unless they are told beforehand of the
reason of this anomoly. In default of being able to
decide between two such dissimilar opinions it seems
that the artist, in such a case, can do no better than
follow his own sentiment; without foolishly straining
after the chimera of popular suffrage.

The phrase in question is of a rhythm extremely
marked; which, afterwards passing to the harmony, is
reproduced in a multitude of aspects without arresting
its cadenced march until the end. The employment
of a rhythmic form in *ostinato* has never been
attempted with so much success; and this allegro, the
extensive development of which runs constantly upon
the same idea, is treated with such inconceivable saga-
city, the changes of tonality are so frequent and ingenious, the chords are formed into groups and
enchainments of such novelty, that the movement concludes before the attention and ardent emotion which

it excites in the listener have had time to lose anything of their extreme vivacity.

The harmonic effect most seriously blamed by the partisans of scholastic discipline, and at the same time the most successful one, is that of the resolution of the discord in the chord of six, five, on the subdominant in the key of E natural. This discord of the second, placed in an upper part against a loud tremolo between the first and second violins, is resolved in a way altogether new. One resolution might have allowed the E to remain, and have caused the F sharp to rise to G; whilst another might have kept the F whilst causing the E to fall to D. Beethoven uses neither one nor the other of these. Without changing his bass he brings the two parts of the discord together, in an octave on F natural, by making the F sharp descend a semitone and the E a major seventh. The chord, therefore, which was previously one of six, five, now becomes a minor sixth; its fifth having disappeared upon F natural. The sudden change from *forte* to *piano* at the precise moment of this singular harmonic transformation both gives it a more decided aspect and renders its grace twofold.

Let us not forget, before passing to the next movement to mention the curious crescendo by means of which Beethoven reintroduces his favourite rhythm, which he had for an instant abandoned. It is produced by a two-bar phrase:

D, C sharp, B sharp, B sharp, C sharp,

in the key of A major; repeated, eleven times in succession, at a low pitch, by the basses and violas; whilst
the wind instruments hold E, above, below and in the
middle, in quadruple octave; and whilst the violins
keep on delivering, as a sort of chime, the notes:

E, A, E, C sharp,

the percussions of which continually increase in speed
and are combined in such a way as to present the
dominant when the basses are at D or B sharp; and
either the tonic or its third whenever they play C sharp.
This is absolutely new; and no imitator has, I think,
yet tried very happily to apply this beautiful discovery.

The rhythm, which is one as simple as that of the
first movement, although of different form, is equally
the principal cause of the incredible effect produced by
the allegretto. It consists exclusively of a dactyl followed by a spomdee; which occur without ceasing,
sometimes in three parts, sometimes in a single one,
and sometimes in the whole of the parts together.
Sometimes they serve as an accompaniment, often
attracting a concentrated attention to themselves, or
furnishing the first theme of a small episodial double
fugue for the stringed instruments. It appears at first
for the lower strings of the violas, violoncellos and
double basses, marked with a simple *piano;* with the
intention of being soon afterwards repeated in a
pianissimo full of melancholy and mystery. From

there it passes to the second violins; whilst the violoncellos chant a sort of lamentation in the minor mode;
the rhythmical phrase continuing to rise from octave
to octave, and thus arriving at the pitch of the first
violins.   These, by a crescendo, transmit it to the wind
instruments in the upper region of the orchestra; where
it then bursts forth in all its force.   Thereupon, the
melodious plaint being stated with greater energy,
assumes the character of a convulsive lamentation;
irreconciliable rhythms painfully agitate one against
another; for these are tears, and sobs and supplications
—in short, the expression of a grief without limit and
of a devouring form of suffering.   But a gleam of
hope has just appeared; these agonising accents being
succeeded by a vapourous melody, pure, simple, soft,
sad and resigned; like *patience smiling at grief.*   Only
the basses continue their inexorable rhythm under this
rainbow of melody; and it seems, if I may borrow a
quotation from English poetry, like:

> One fatal remembrance, one sorrow, that throws
> Its black shade alike o'er our joys and our woes.

After a few alternations remindful of anguish and
resignation the orchestra, as if fatigued by such a painful struggle, presents only fragments of the original
theme, and dies away exhausted.   The flutes and oboes
take up the theme with a murmuring voice, but strength
fails them to finish it; and it is the violins to whom
the termination falls, in a few notes of *pizzicato,*

scarcely perceptible. Afterwards, with a flicker of fresh animation, remindful of the flame of a lamp which is about to die out, the wind instruments exhale a profound sigh upon an indecisive harmony, and *all is silence*. This plaintive exclamation, with which the andante both commences and concludes, is produced by a chord (that of the 6-4) which has a continual tendency to resolve upon some other; and the incomplete harmonic sense of which is the only one which could permit its use for the purpose of finishing in such a way as to leave the hearer with a vague impression and to augment the feeling of dreamy sadness in which the whole of the preceding must necessarily have plunged him.

The subject of the Scherzo is modelled in quite a new style. It is in F major; and, instead of concluding its first section in C, or B flat, or D minor, or A minor, or A flat, or D flat, after the habit of the great majority of pieces of this kind, it is upon the key of its *third*—or in other words upon A natural major—that the modulation at last falls. The scherzo of the "Pastoral" symphony, which is also in F, modulates into D major a third lower. There is some resemblance in the colour presented by this contrast of keys; but this is not the only affinity to be observed as existing between the two works. The trio of the present movement *(presto meno assai)*, in which the violins hold the dominant almost continually, whilst the oboes and clarinets execute a genial rustic melody

below, is altogether within the sentiment of the landscape and the idyll. We meet in it also a new form
of *crescendo*, stated in a lower part by the second horn,
which murmurs the two notes

A, G sharp

in duple rhythm, although the bar is of three beats;
and accentuates the G sharp, although A is the in-
tegral note. The public seems always struck with
astonishment on hearing this passage.

The finale is at least as rich as the preceding movements in new combinations, piquant modulations and
capricious charm. The theme presents a certain relation with that of the overture of "Armide"; but it is
only in the arrangement of the first few notes, and is
more evident to the eye than to the ear; for, when
executed, nothing can be more dissimilar than these
two ideas. We should better appreciate the freshness
and coquetry of Beethoven's phrase, so different from
the cavalier-like spirit of Gluck's theme, if the chords
taken in upper parts by the wind instruments were less
dominating over the first violins singing in the medium
register, whilst the second violins and violas accompany the melody below with a *tremolo* in double-
stopping. Throughout the course of this finale Beethoven has drawn effects as graceful as they are unforeseen from the sudden transition from the key of
C sharp minor to that of D major. One of his
happiest bold harmonic strokes is unquestionably the

great pedal on the dominant E ; set off by a D sharp of a value equal to that of the principal note. The chord of the seventh is also sometimes introduced above in such a way that the D natural of the upper parts falls precisely upon the D sharp of the basses. One might expect the result of this to be a horrible discord; or, at all events, a deficiency of clearness in the harmony. Nothing of the kind happens, however; for the tonal force of this dominant is such that the D sharp does not affect it in any way, and the bourdon of E continues exclusively to be heard. Beethoven did not write his music for the mere purpose of being looked at.

The coda which is introduced by this threatening pedal is of extraordinary brightness, and well worthy of terminating such a masterpiece—alike of technical ability taste, fantasy, knowledge and inspiration.

SYMPHONY NO. 8, IN F.

SYMPHONY NO. 8, IN F.

THIS symphony is in F, like the "Pastorale"; but conceived within proportions less vast than its predecessors. However, if it scarcely surpasses in respect of amplitude of form the first symphony in C, it is, at all events, far superior to it in the threefold respect of instrumentation, rhythm and melodic style.

The first movement contains two subjects; both being gentle and calm in character. The second, which, in our opinion, is the more remarkable, seems continually to avoid the perfect cadence; by modulating first of all, in a totally unexpected manner (the phrase begins in D and finishes in C), and afterwards, in disappearing, without any conclusion, on the chord of the diminished seventh.

To hear this melodic caprice it would almost seem as if the author, though desiring a gentle emotion, had been suddenly prevented from continuing his joyous song by the intervention of some sad idea.

The andante scherzando is one of those productions for which it would be equally vain to seek either a model or a counterpart; which seem to have fallen from heaven, and to have straightway entered the author's mind; which he therefore writes, as it were, at a stroke; and which we can only listen to, amazed. The wind instruments here play a part which is the opposite of that which usually falls to their lot. In other words they accompany, with added chords, repeated eight times *pianissimo* in each bar, the lightsome dialogue *a punta d'arco* of the violins and basses. It is soft and ingenuous, besides being of an indolence specially graceful; like the song of two children gathering flowers in a meadow on a beautiful spring morning.

The principal phrase is formed of two sections of three bars each, the symmetrical disposition of which is disturbed by the silence which follows the bass reply. It thus happens that the first section finishes upon a weak, and the second upon a strong, beat. The chord-repetitions of oboe, clarinets, horns and bassoons are so interesting that the listener seems to be prevented from noticing the symmetrical defect produced in the *cantabile* of the string instruments by the amount of added silence.

The addition alluded to evidently exists only for the purpose of allowing the delightful chord from which the happy melody is next to take its flight to be somewhat longer heard alone. We see again, by this example, that the law of strict outline may sometimes be infringed with success; but can it be believed that this ravishing idyll concludes by the very one of all

common features for which Beethoven had the greatest
aversion? viz., by the Italian cadence. At the moment
when the instrumental conversation of the two little
orchestras, wind and string, is most attractive, the composer, as if he had been suddenly *compelled* to finish,
makes the violins play in *tremolo* the four notes:

G	F	A	B flat
sixth	dominant	leading note	tonic

repeàts them several times precipitately, for all the
world as the Italians do when they sing

Fe - li - ci - tà,

and then—stops short! I have never been able to
explain to myself this comical wind-up.

A minuet, with all the cut and precise movement of
the minuets of Haydn, here takes the place of the
scherzo in quick triple time which Beethoven invented;
and of which he made such ingenious and attractive
use in all his other symphonic compositions. To speak
truly, this movement is but ordinary; and the antiquity
of the form seems somehow to have stifled the composer's thought.

The finale, on the contrary, sparkles with life; its
ideas being brilliant, new and luxuriously developed.
There are to be found diatonic progressions, in two
parts and in contrary motion, serving the composer as
means for a crescendo of immense extent and grand

effect for his peroration. The harmony merely includes a few cases of harshness; produced by the resolution of passing-notes not being sufficiently prompt, and by the passing-notes occasionally stopping short before a rest.

By somewhat straining the mere letter of theoretical law these passing discords can easily be explained; but, in performance, they always produce a more or less unpleasant effect. A contrary instance is afforded by the high pedal of the flutes and oboes on F; whilst the drums, tuned in the octave, hammer out the same note below, at the re-entry of the theme; the violins playing:

C, G, B flat,

of the chord of the dominant seventh, preceded by the third—F, A, fragment of the tonic chord. I hold that this sustained upper note, which is forbidden theoretically, as it forms no part of the harmony, gives no offence. Far from that, thanks to an adroit disposition of the instruments and to the peculiar character of the phrase the result of this aggregation of sound is excellent, and of remarkable sweetness.

We must not omit to mention, before concluding, a certain orchestral effect—the one of all perhaps which most surprises the listener at the performance of this finale. We allude to the note, C sharp, which is loudly struck by the entire mass of instruments in unison and octave after a diminuendo which has just died away upon C natural. This roar of sound is immediately followed, on the first two occasions, by a return of the theme in F. This shows that the C sharp was enharmonically really a D flat, chromatically altered from the sixth note of the scale. But the third appearance of this strange return bears a different aspect. The orchestra having modulated to C, as before, now strikes a *genuine* D flat; followed by a fragment of the theme in that key. Then comes an equally *genuine* C sharp; succeeded by another portion of the theme in C sharp minor. Resuming now the same C sharp, and repeating it three times with increase of force, the entire theme now enters—in F sharp minor.

The same sound, therefore, which had figured at the beginning as a minor sixth, becomes successively at its last appearance :

1. Tonic, major, flattened.
2. Tonic, minor, flattened.
3. Dominant.

All this is very curious.

SYMPHONY NO. 9, IN D MINOR.

(THE "CHORAL.")

SYMPHONY NO. 9, IN D MINOR.
(THE "CHORAL.")

TO analyse such a composition is a difficult and
dangerous task, and one which we have long hesi-
tated to undertake. It is a hazardous attempt, excuse for
which can only lie in persevering efforts to place ourselves at the composer's point of view and thus perceive the inner sense of his work, feel its effect, and
study the impressions which it has so far produced;
both upon privileged organisations and upon the
public at large. Amongst the many judgments which
have been passed upon this work there are perhaps not
even two which are identical. It is regarded by some
critics as a *monstrous folly*. Others can only see in it
the parting gleams of an expiring genius. A few,
more prudent, confess that they do not yet understand
it; but are hopeful of being able to appreciate it, at
least approximately, later on. The great bulk of
artists deem it to be an extraordinary conception;
though some of its parts are not yet explained, and
appear to have no direct object.

But there are a few musicians who are impelled by

their nature to bestow every care in examining whatever may tend to increase the field of art. These have
ripely reflected upon the general plan of the "Choral"
Symphony; and, after having read it and attentively
listened to it on many occasions, they are firm in the
conviction that this work forms the most magnificent
expression of Beethoven's genius. That opinion, as
we have already hinted in these pages, is the one to
which we adhere.

Without prying into what the composer may have
wished to express in the way of ideas personal to
himself in this vast musical poem, this being a search
in favour of which the field of conjecture is equally
open to everyone, let us see if the novelty of form is
not here justified by an intention altogether independent of philosophic or religious thought, an intention as reasonable and beautiful for the fervent
Christian as for the Pantheist or Atheist—an intention,
in fact, purely musical and poetical.

Beethoven had already written eight symphonies
before this. What means were open to him, in the
event of his purposing to go beyond the point at which
he had already arrived, by the unaided resources of
instrumentation? *The junction of vocal with instrumental forces.* But, in order to observe the law of
crescendo, and to place the power of the auxiliary
which he wished to give the orchestra in effective relief
in the work itself, was it not necessary still to allow
the instruments to occupy the foreground of the picture

which he proposed to unfold? This proposition being once admitted, we can easily imagine him induced to adopt a style of mixed music capable of serving as connecting link between the two great divisions of the symphony. It was the instrumental "recitative" which thus became the bridge which he ventured to throw out between chorus and orchestra; and over which the instruments passed to attain a junction with the voices.

The passage being decided on, the author was obliged to make his intention clear by announcing the fusion which he was about to effect. Then it was that, speaking by the mouth of a Coryphée, he himself cried out, in employing the very notes of the instrumental recitative which he had just employed:

O Freunde, nicht diese Töne! sondern lasst uns augenehmere anstimmen, und freudenvollere.*

In the above lies, so to speak, the "treaty of alliance" entered into between chorus and orchestra; the same phrase of recitative pronounced by one and the other seeming to be the form of an oath mutually taken. From that point, the musician was free in the choice of the text of his choral composition. It is to Schiller that Beethoven applies. He takes the poet's

---

* "O Friends, not tones like these! But let us turn to others, more pleasant and full of joy."
Berlioz's rendering is as under:
"Amis! plus de pareils accords, mais commençons des chants plus agréable, et plus remplis de joie." These words are not Schiller's but Beethoven's. (Translator's note.)

"Ode to Joy," colours it with a thousand tints which the unaided poetry could never have conveyed, and, right up to the end, he pursues one continual road of increasing pomp and grandeur and éclat.

Such is, probably, the reason, more or less plausible, of the general arrangement of this immense composition; the several parts of which we are now about to study.

The first movement, with its imprint of sombre majesty, does not resemble any which Beethoven had previously written. The harmony is sometimes of an excessive boldness; and designs of the most original kind as well as features of the most expressive order meet, cross and interlace in all ways without producing either obscurity or encumbrance. On the contrary, the general result is *one* effect which is perfectly clear. The multitude of orchestral voices may complain or threaten, each one in its own peculiar way or special style. But they all seem to unite in forming one single voice; so great is the force of the sentiment by which they are animated.

This *allegro maestoso*, written in D minor, commences, however, upon the chord of A without its third; or, in other words, with a continuation of the notes A, E, placed as a fifth, and arpeggioed above and below by the first violins, violas and double basses, so that the listener does not know whether what he hears is the chord of A minor, that of A major, or that of the dominant of D. This prolonged indecision as regards tonality gives much force and dignity of character to the entry of the *tutti* on the chord of D minor. The peroration contains accents which move the soul completely; and it would be difficult to find anything more profoundly tragic that this song of the wind instruments under which a chromatic phrase in *tremolo* for the stringed instruments gradually swells and rises —grumbling the while, like the sea at approach of a storm.   This is indeed a magnificent inspiration.

We shall have more than one occasion in course of this work to draw attention to aggregations of notes to which it is really impossible to give the name of chords, and it is as well to admit that the reason of these anomalies escapes us completely.   Thus, at page 17[*] of the admirable movement of which we have just spoken, there is a melodic design for clarinets and bassoons, in the key of C minor, which is accompanied in the following way:

1. The bass takes F sharp (with diminished seventh harmony).

2. Then, A flat (with chord of three, four and augmented sixth).

3. Lastly, G (above which the flutes and oboes strike the notes, E flat, G, C, yielding a chord of six, four).

---

[*] As the page here indicated will naturally fail to correspond with editions of the work at present in use, the reader desirous of identifying the passage referred to must be entirely guided by its description.   (Translator's note.)

No. 3 would thus correctly resolve No. 2 if the second violins and violas did not persist in adding to the harmony the two notes, F and A flat; which so pervert it as to produce a very disagreeable confusion, though happily very short.

This passage is but lightly instrumented and is of a character altogether free from roughness; for which reason I cannot understand this quadruple discord, so strangely introduced without cause. One might suspect an engraver's error; but, on examining these two bars and those which precede them, all doubt disappears; and the conviction arises that such was really the intention of the composer.

The *scherzo vivace* which follows contains nothing similar. We find in it, it is true, several pedals, both high and medium on the tonic; and which pass through the chord of the dominant. But I have already made my profession of faith on the subject of these holding-notes foreign to the harmony; and there is no need of this new example to prove the excellent help which can be drawn therefrom when they are naturally induced by the musical sense. It is by means of the rhythm especially that Beethoven has been able to imbue this charming *badinage* with so much interest. The theme, so full of vivacity when it presents itself with its fugal reply at a distance of four bars, literally sparkles with life, later on; when, the answer coming in a bar sooner than expected, by that means forms a three-bar rhythmic design, in lieu of the duple rhythm of the commencement.

The middle of the scherzo is taken up by a *presto à deux temps* (alla breve) of quite a country-like joviality, and of which the theme unfolds itself upon the intermediary pedals, either of tonic or dominant, and with accompaniment of a counter-melody which also harmonises equally well with one or other of these two holding-notes. The song is introduced for the last time by an oboe phrase of delightful freshness; which, after having toyed for some time with the chord of the major ninth (dominant of D) disports itself in the key of F in a manner as graceful as it is unexpected. In this may be perceived a reflection of those gentle impressions so dear to Beethoven—impressions produced by the aspect of Nature smiling and calm, the purity of the air, or the first rays of dawn on a spring morning.

In the adagio cantabile the principle of unity is so little observed that it might rather be regarded as two distinct pieces than as one. The first melody, in B flat and in common time, is succeeded by another melody, absolutely different from it, in triple time, and in D. Then the first theme, slightly altered and varied by the first violins, makes a second appearance in the original key, for the purpose of reintroducing the triple melody. This now appears without either alteration or variation in the key of G; after which the first theme definitively installs itself, and does not again permit its rival subject to share with it the attention of the listener.

Several hearings are necessary before one can altogether become accustomed to so singular a disposition of this marvellous adagio. As to the beauty of all these melodies, the infinite grace of the ornaments applied to them, the sentiments of melancholy tenderness of passionate sadness and of religious meditation which they express, if my prose could give of all this even an approximate idea, music would have found in the "written word" such a competitor as even the greatest of all poets was never able to oppose to it. It is an immense work; and, when once its powerful charm has been experienced, the only answer for the critic who reproaches the composer for having violated the law of unity is:

So much the worse for the law!

We are now approaching the moment when the vocal and orchestral elements are to be united. The violoncellos and double basses intone the recitative, of which we have already spoken, after a ritornello of the wind instruments as violent and rough as a cry of anger. The chord of the major sixth (F, A, D) with which this presto starts off is intruded upon by an appoggiatura on the B flat, struck at the same time by flutes, oboes and clarinets. This sixth note of the key of D minor grates horribly against the dominant and produces an excessively harsh effect. This is well ex-

pressive of fury and rage; but I still do not quite see
what it was that excited the composer to this sentiment, unless, before saying to his Coryphée:

Let us turn to other tones more pleasant and full of joy,

he wanted, in virtue of some odd whim, to calumniate
instrumental harmony.

He seems to regret it, however, for, between each
phrase of the bass recitative, he quotes, as souvenirs
held in affection, fragments of the three preceding
movements; and, moreover, after this same recitative,
he places in the orchestra, amid an exquisite choice of
chords, the beautiful theme which all the voices are
shortly about to sing to the ode of Schiller. This
chant, of calm and gentle character, becomes gradually
more animated and brilliant in passing from the
basses, who first announce it, to the violins and wind
instruments. After a sudden interruption, the entire
orchestra resumes the furious ritornello already mentioned, which now announces the vocal recitative.

The first chord is again placed on F; which is
supposed to carry third and sixth. It does really carry
them; but, this time, the composer is not contented with
the appoggiatura B flat, for he adds E, G and C sharp,
so that

ALL THE NOTES OF THE MINOR DIATONIC SCALE

are played together, and produce the frightful
assemblage:

F, A, C sharp, E, G, B flat, D.

The French composer Martin, says Martini, wanted,
in his opera of "Sappho," about forty years ago, to
produce an analogous effect by employing, all at once,
every diatonic, chromatic and enharmonic interval.
This happens at the moment when Phaon's lover is
about to throw herself into the waves; and, without
troubling about the suitability of such an attempt, and
without asking whether or no this venture was an in-
fringement of the dignity of art, we may be sure, at
all events, that his object was not misunderstood. My
efforts to discover that of Beethoven would, however,
be completely useless. I perceive a formal intention—
a calculated and thought-out project—to produce two
discords at the two instants which precede the successive appearances of vocal and instrumental recitative.
But, though I have sought high and low for the reason
of this idea, I am forced to avow that it is unknown to
me.

The Coryphée, after having sung his recitative, the
words of which, as we have said, are by Beethoven himself, alone delivers the theme of the "Ode to Joy," to
the light accompaniment of two wind instruments and
strings pizzicato.

This theme appears right up to the end of the symphony; and is always recognisable, although its aspect
changes continually. The study of these various
transformations presents an interest so much the more
powerful as each one of them gives a new and decided
tint to the expression of one and the same sentiment—

that of joy. This joy is, at first, full of gentleness and peace; but becomes somewhat more lively at the moment when the female voices make themselves heard. The time changes; the phrase first sung in common time now appears in 6-8 and, with continual syncopation; when it assumes a stronger character; becomes more agile; and, generally, approaches a warlike style.

This is the song of the hero sure of victory; we can almost see his armour sparkle and hear the sound of his measured step. A fugato theme, in which the original melodic design may still be traced, serves for a while as material for orchestral disportment—this representing the various movements of a crowd, active and full of ardour.

But the chorus soon returns, forcibly chanting the joyous hymn in its first simplicity; aided by the wind, which repeats the chords in following the melody; and traversed, in many ways, by a diatonic design, executed by the entire mass of strings, in unison and octave.

The andante maestoso which follows is a kind of chorale; first intoned by the tenors and basses of the chorus with one trombone, violoncellos and basses. The joy is now religious, grave and immense. The choir ceases for a moment, in order to resume its wide harmony with a lesser strength, after an orchestral solo producing an organ effect of great beauty. The imitation of the majestic instrument of Christian churches is produced by the flute lower register, the clarinet chalumeau, the lower sounds of the bassoon, the violas divided into high and medium parts, and the violon-cellos playing upon their open strings G, D or upon C open string with its octave.

This movement begins in G; passing into C and then into F, and finishing by an organ-point on the domin-ant seventh of D. Following it is a grand allegro in 6-4 in which, from the very beginning, the first theme, already so variously produced, and the chorale of the preceding andante appear united. The contrast of these two ideas is rendered even more salient by a rapid variation of the joyous song, which is executed below the long notes of the chorale, not only by the first violins, but also by the double basses.

Now, it is impossible for double basses to execute a succession of notes so rapid; and no one has yet been able to explain how a man so skilful as Beethoven in the art of instrumentation could possibly forget him-self so far as to write for this heavy instrument a feature of this kind.

There is less manliness, less grandeur and more lightness of style in the next movement; the substance of which presents a simple gaiety, first expressed by four voices alone, and afterwards warmly coloured by addition of the chorus.

Some tender and religious accents alternate, twice successively, with this gay melody; but the movement increases in precipitation. The whole orchestra breaks out; and percussion instruments, including kettledrums, cymbals, triangle and bass drum rudely mark the strong beats of the bar. Joy resumes dominion— popular and tumultuous joy, which would even resemble an orgy did not the whole of the voices, in terminating, pause anew upon a solemn rhythm, in order to send their last salute of love and respect to religious joy by an ecstatic exclamation. The orchestra finishes alone; but not without projecting from its ardent course fragments of the first theme, of which one cannot tire.

A translation as exact as possible of the German poetry treated by Beethoven will now give the reader the key to this multitude of musical combinations, skilled auxiliaries of a sustained inspiration, docile instruments of a powerful and indefatigable genius.

It is as follows:

O joy! beautiful god-like spark, daughter of Elysium, we enter thy sanctuary all ardent with divine fire! Thy magic power unites again those whom the world keeps strictly apart; under the shadow of thy wing all men become brothers.

He who has the happiness to be friend of a friend, he who possesses a good woman; yes, he who can call even one soul on this earth his own, let him mix his joy with ours! But let the man to whom this has not been granted steal away from us, in weeping.

All beings drink of joy at the bosom of Nature; the good and the wicked follow their flowery ways. From Nature we have kisses and wine and a friend proved in death. She has given pleasure to the worm; the cherubim stands before God.

Gay, as the suns revolve in the vast heavenly expanse, so, brethren, follow your way, full of joy, like the hero who marches to victory.

Let millions of beings embrace; may this kiss reach the entire world! Brethren, beyond the stars there must dwell a dear Father.

Millions, do ye prostrate yourselves? World, dost thou recognise the Creator? Seek Him above the canopy of the stars! There is His dwelling-place.*

* * * * * *

This symphony is the most difficult of all by this composer; its performance necessitating study, both patient and repeated; but, above all, well directed. It requires, moreover, a number of singers greater than would otherwise be necessary; as the chorus is evidently supposed to cover the orchestra in many places; and, also, because the manner in which the music is set to the words and the excessive height of some of the vocal parts render voice production difficult, and diminish the volume and energy of the sounds produced.

* Berlioz's version is as follows:

O Joie! belle étincelle des dieux, fille de l'Elysée, nous entrons tout brûlants du feu divin dans ton sanctuaire! un pouvoir magique réunit ceux que le monde et le rang séparent; à l'ombre de ton aile si douce tous les hommes deviennent frères.

Celui qui a le bonheur d'être devenu l'ami d'un ami; celui qui possède une femme aimable; oui, celui qui peut dire à soi une âme sur cette terre, que sa joie se mêle à la nôtre! mais que l'homme à qui cette félicité ne fut pas accordée se glisse en pleurant hors au lieu qui nous rassemble!

Tous les êtres boivent la joie au sein de la nature; les bons et les méchants suivent des chemins de fleurs. La nature nous a donné l'amour, le vin et la mort, cette preuve de l'amitié. Elle a donné la volupté au ver; le chérubin est debout devan Dieu.

Gai! gai! comme les soleils roulent sur le plan magnifique du ciel, de même. frères, courez fournir votre carrière, pleins de joie comme le héros qui marche à la victoire.

Que des millions d'êtres, que le monde entier se confonde dans un même embrassement! Frères, au delà des sphères doit habiter un père bien-ainé.

Millions, vous, vous prosternez? reconnaissez-vous l'œuvre du Créateur; Cherchez l'auteur de ces merveilles au-dessus des astres, car c'est là qu'il réside.

Whatever may be said, it is certain that Beethoven, when finishing his work, and when contemplating the majestic dimensions of the monument he had just erected, might very well have said to himself :

Let Death come now, my task is accomplished.

A FEW WORDS ON THE TRIOS AND SONATAS OF BEETHOVEN.

A FEW WORDS ON THE TRIOS AND SONATAS OF BEETHOVEN.

THERE are many people in France for whom the name of Beethoven awakens ideas only of the Orchestra and of the Symphony. They do not know that, in every style of music, this indefatigable Titan has left behind him masterpieces of almost equal excellence.

He has written an opera, "Fidelio"; a ballet, "Prometheus"; a melodrama, "Egmont"; tragedy-overtures: those of "Coriolan" and "The Ruins of Athens"; six or seven other overtures on indeterminate subjects; two great masses; an oratorio, "Mount of Olives"; eighteen string quartets; several other quartets and quintets for three or four wind instruments and piano; trios for piano, violin and 'cello; a great number of sonatas for piano alone or for piano with violin or 'cello; a septet for four string and three wind instruments; a great violin concerto; four or five piano concertos with orchestra; a fantasia for piano, orchestra and chorus; a multitude of variations for different instruments; songs and romances with piano accompaniment; a collection of hymns for one or several voices; a cantata or lyric scena with orchestra; choruses with orchestra on different German poems; two volumes of harmony and counterpoint studies; and, to wind up with, the nine famous symphonies.

It must not be supposed that this fecundity of Beethoven has anything in common with that of the Italian composers, who only reckon their works by the fifty; as, for instance, the hundred and sixty scores of Paisiello. Certainly not; such an idea would be terribly unjust. If we except "The Ruins of Athens" overture, and, perhaps, two or three other fragments really unworthy of the great name they bear, and which only fell from their composer's pen at those rare moments of drowsiness which Horace reproaches with a certain irony to good Homer himself, everything else is in the noble, elevated, firm, bold, expressive, poetical and always *new* style which, without question, renders Beethoven the sentinel in advance of musical civilisation.

It is quite as much as can be said if, in this great number of compositions, one may discover a few vague resemblances between some of the thousands of phrases which form their splendour and their life. This astonishing faculty of being always *new*, without departing from what is true and beautiful, can be understood to a certain point in pieces of a lively movement. The thought is then aided by a rhythmic resource; and can, in its capricious bounds, more easily escape from the beaten track. But where we fail to understand it is in the adagios—in those extra-human meditations into which the Pantheistic genius of Beethoven so loves to plunge itself. Then, there is no more passion; no more earthly pictures or hymns, either to joy, love or glory. No more childish songs or gentle talk; no more sallies, whether bitter or grotesque; nor any more of those terrible bursts of fury—those accents of hatred, which the pangs of a secret suffering so often compel. He has no longer even disdain in his heart, for he is no longer of our kind. He has forgotten it; and, no longer in our atmosphere, but calm and solitary, swimming in the ether, he is like those eagles of the Andes who wing through space at heights below in which other creatures would find nothing but asphyxia and death. His glances are directed into space; and he flies towards the suns, singing the praise of infinite nature.

Are we to believe that the genius of this man was able to take such a flight, so to speak, whenever he liked? We may convince ourselves of that, however, by the numerous proofs which he has left; less in his symphonies than in his compositions for piano alone. There, and only there, having no longer a numerous audience in view, such as the public or the crowd, he seems to have written only for himself, with that majestic abandonment which the bulk of people do not understand, and which the necessity of promptly arriving at what we call "effect" must inevitably spoil. There, also, the task of the executant becomes exacting; if not by the difficulties of mechanism, at least by the great intelligence and profound sentiment which such works require from him. The virtuose must, at all cost, efface himself before the composer; after the manner of the orchestra in the symphonies. There must be complete absorption of one by the other. But it is precisely by identifying himself in this way with the thought which he transmits to us that the interpreter rises to the entire height of his model.

There is a work of Beethoven known by the name of "Sonata in C sharp minor," the adagio of which is one of those poetical productions which human language cannot describe. The means employed are extremely simple; for the left hand merely displays some wide chords of a sadly solemn character, holding each one sufficiently long for the vibrations of the strings to die away; whilst the right employs its lower fingers to arpeggio an *ostinato* accompaniment, the form of which scarcely varies from end to end; and during which the other fingers cause a sort of lamentation to be heard—the melodic efflorescence of a sombre harmony. One day, about thirty years ago, Liszt was executing this adagio before a few friends of whom I was one; and he took upon himself to distort it somewhat, after the manner which he had then adopted in order to make himself applauded by the fashionable public; and, instead of the long sustainings of the bass and severe uniformity of rhythm and movement of

which I have just spoken, he used shakes and tremolos
—he hurried and slackened the time—thus disturbing,
by passionate accents, the calm of that sadness; and
causing the roll of thunder to issue from that cloudless
sky, which was but slightly overcast by the setting sun.

This caused me to suffer cruelly, I avow; even more
than it has ever happened to me to suffer on hearing
those wretched singers of ours embellish the grand air
in "Der Freischütz"; for, added to the torture, was
the chagrin of seeing such an artist fall into the pit
which is generally reserved for mediocrities.

But, what could be done? Liszt was then just like
those children who, without complaint, get up after a
fall (which we have to pretend not to see); and who
would burst into tears if anyone held a hand to them.
And grandly did he get up again; for, a few years
afterwards, it was no longer he who was pursuing success, but success which was running itself out of breath
in pursuit of him : the tables were turned.

We must now return to our sonata. Recently, one
of those men of heart and mind whom artists are so
happy to meet had gathered a few friends, and I was
of the number. Liszt arrived during the evening; and,
finding the conversation turning upon the value of a
piece by Weber, which, whether by reason of an indifferent performance or from some other cause, the
public had received rather badly, he took his seat at
the piano in order to reply to the antagonists of
Weber in his own way.

The argument seemed to admit of no reply; and everyone was constrained to confess that a work of genius had been misunderstood. As Liszt finished, the lamp seemed about to go out; and one of the company was preparing to light it again.

"Don't do so," said I, "if he will only play us the C sharp minor adagio of Beethoven, the faint light will certainly not spoil it."

"With pleasure," said Liszt, "only, put out the light altogether, and screen the fire; let us have complete darkness."

Then, in the obscurity, and after a moment's composure, the noble elegy—the same which formerly he had so strangely distorted, appeared in all its sublime simplicity. Not a note or emphasis was added to what the composer had written. It was the shade of Beethoven, brought forth by the virtuose, and whose great voice we heard. Each one of us was trembling in silence; and, after the last chord, no one stirred—for it had moved us to tears.

A somewhat considerable portion of the French public, however, knows nothing of the existence of these marvellous works. Certainly, the entire trio in B flat, the adagio of the one in D and the Sonata in A for piano and 'cello should have proved to those to whom they are familiar that the great composer is far from having devoted all the treasures of his genius to orchestra alone.

But this is not his last word: for that we must go

to the sonatas for piano alone. The moment will perhaps soon come when these works, which are ahead of all that is most advanced in art, will be understood, if not by the crowd, at least by a select public. This is an experience to be tested; but, should it not succeed, it must be tried again later.

The great sonatas of Beethoven form a good guage wherewith to measure the development of our own musical intelligence.

"FIDELIO."

"FIDELIO."

Opera in Three Acts by Beethoven.
The Production at the Theatre Lyrique.

ON the first ventôse, of the year VI, the theatre of the Rue Feydeau produced, for the first time, "Leonora, or Conjugal Love; historic fact, in two acts" (for such was the title of the piece); words by M. Bouilly, music by P. Gaveaux. The work appeared to be only second-rate, notwithstanding the talent displayed by the actors of the principal parts. These were Gaveaux, the composer of the music; and Madame Scio, a great actress of that time.

Several years afterwards Paer wrote a graceful score to an Italian libretto of which the Leonora of M. Bouilly was again the heroine; and it was in coming away from a representation of this work that Beethoven, with the uncouth humour habitual to him, said to Paer:

"I like your play. I have a good mind to set it to music."

Such was the origin of the masterpiece which we have now to consider. The first appearance of the "Fidelio" of Beethoven on the German stage did not forbode the future celebrity of that work; and it is said that the representations of it were soon suspended. Some time afterwards, however, it reappeared; modified in several ways, both as to music and text; and furnished with a new overture. This second trial was a complete success; and Beethoven, loudly recalled by the audience, was brought upon the stage after the first act, and again after the second act; the finale of which produced an enthusiasm hitherto unknown at Vienna. The score of "Fidelio" was, however, none the less subject to varying degrees of bitter criticism; but, dating from that moment, it was performed on every stage in Germany; where it has, ever since, maintained its position; and where it now forms part of the classical repertoire. The London theatres, somewhat later, extended to it the same honour; and, in 1827, upon the occasion of a German troupe coming to represent it at Paris, "Fidelio," the two principal parts in which were sung with rare talent by Hailzinger and Madame Schrœder-Devrient, was welcomed with enthusiasm. It has just been placed upon the Theâtre-Lyrique; a fortnight ago it was appearing on that of Covent Garden in London; and, at the present moment, they are playing it in New York. Tell me, if you can, at what theatres the "Leonora," either of Gaveaux or of Paer, is now being performed. It is only the book-worms who even know of the existence of these two operas. They are done with; and exist no more. The fact is that, of these three scores, the first is extremely weak; the second scarcely a work of talent; and the third a masterpiece of genius.

In fact, the more I hear, and the more I read, Beethoven's work, the more I find it worthy of admiration. The general effect and the details of it appear to me equally beautiful; for, everywhere, energy, grandeur, originality and a sentiment as profound as it is true is to be found revealed.

It belongs to that powerful race of calumniated works upon which are outpoured the most inconceivable prejudices, and the most manifest falsehoods; but the vitality of which is so intense that nothing can prevail against it. Like those vigorous beeches, born amid rocks and ruins, which finish by splitting the rocks and piercing the walls, and which rise at last, proud and verdant, all the more solidly implanted on account of the obstacles they have had to overcome in order to emerge; whilst the willows which grew without any trouble upon the river bank, fall into its bed, and perish forgotten.

Beethoven wrote four overtures for his one opera. After having finished the first one he began it again, without anyone knowing exactly why; retaining the general disposition and all the subjects, but joining them by different modulations, scoring them anew, and

adding a crescendo effect and a flute solo. This solo
is not, in my opinion, worthy of the great style of the
rest of the work. The composer, however, seems to
have preferred this second version—since it was the
first published. The manuscript of the other one
remained in possession of M. Schindler, a friend of
the composer; and was published, only ten years ago,
at the house of Richaut. I have had the honour of
conducting it some twenty times at Drury Lane
Theatre in London, and at a few concerts in Paris; its
effect being both grand and exciting. The second
version, however, has preserved the popularity which
it acquired under the name of "overture to Leonora";
and it will probably keep it.

This superb overture, perhaps the most beautiful of
Beethoven, shared the fate of several numbers of the
opera; and was suppressed after the first representations. Another (also in C, like the two others), of
charming and gentle character, but the conclusion of
which did not seem calculated to excite applause, met
with no better fortune. Finally, the composer wrote,
for the revival of his opera in modified form, the Overture in E; known by the name of overture to "Fidelio,"
and which was definitively adopted, in preference to
either of the three others. It is a masterful piece, possessed of incomparable life and light, a real symphonic *chef d'œuvre*; but one which does not fit, either
by its character or its material, the opera to which it
serves as an introduction. The other overtures, on the

contrary, are, to some extent, the opera of "Fidelio" abridged; they present, together with the tender accents of Leonora, the sorrowful plaint of the prisoner dying of hunger; the delightful melodies of the trio of the last act; the distant fanfare of the trumpet announcing the arrival of the minister who is to deliver Florestan; in fact, they palpitate with dramatic interest, and are real *overtures to "Fidelio."*

*   *   *   *   *   *

The principal theatres of Germany and England, having perceived, after thirty or forty years, that the second overture of "Leonora" (the first published) was a magnificent work, perform it now as an entr'acte between the first and second acts, whilst keeping the Overture in E for the actual opening. It is a pity that the Theâtre-Lyrique has not thought fit to follow this example. We should even like to see the conservatoire do the same as Mendelssohn did at a Gewandhaus concert at Leipzig; and give us, at one of its séances, the whole of the four overtures of Beethoven's opera.

But this, most likely, would appear an experiment too bold for Paris (why!); and boldness, we know, is not a defect of our musical institutions.

The subject of "Fidelio" (for something must be said about the piece itself) is sad and melodramatic, and has contributed not a little to nourish the prejudice of the French public against this opera. The

story is of a state-prisoner whom the governor of a
fortress desires to starve in his dungeon.   The
prisoner's wife, Leonora, disguised as a young boy,
ingratiates herself with Rocko, the jailer, as a servant,
under the name of Fidelio.   Marceline is the daughter
of Rocko, and is engaged to the turnkey, Jacquino;
but, falling in love with the enticing appearance of
Fidelio, she soon neglects her vulgar swain in favour
of the new-comer.   Pizarre, the governor, impatient
for the death of his victim, and not finding hunger
sufficiently swift in action, resolves to go and strangle
him where he lies.   Order is given to Rocko to dig a
hole in the corner of the dungeon; where the prisoner's
body is shortly to be thrown.

Rocko chooses Fidelio to help him in this ghastly
task; and the poor woman is anguished at thus finding
herself near her husband, who is ready to succumb,
and whom she dare not approach.   Soon, the cruel
Pizarre presents himself; the shackled prisoner gets
up, perceives his executioner, and challenges him; when
Pizarre rushes forward with a dagger in his hand, just
as Fidelio, throwing herself between them, draws a
pistol from her bosom and presents it to the face of
Pizarre, who starts back in fright.

At that very moment a trumpet is heard in the distance.   It is the signal to lower the portcullis and open
the gate of the fortress.   The arrival of the minister
is announced, the governor is prevented from finishing
his work of blood, he rushes from the dungeon, and

the prisoner is saved.   The fact is that, when the minister appears, he recognises in the victim of Pizarre his friend Florestan, upon which there is general delight; though all to the confusion of poor Marceline, who, learning that Fidelio is a woman, goes back to Jacquino.

They have thought it advisable at the Theâtre-Lyrique to trace, over the situations of this piece of M. Bouilly, an altogether new drama.   The scene of the latter is laid at Milan, in 1495; its principal characters being Ludovic Sforza, Jean Galleas, his wife, Isabella of Aragon and Charles VIII, King of France. They have been thus enabled to conclude with a brilliant tableau, set off by costumes brighter than those of the original piece.   That, at all events, was the only reason, poor as it was, which induced M. Carvalho, the able director of this theatre, at the time that "Fidelio" was being rehearsed, to desire such a substitution.   In France they do not admit that a foreign opera should be purely and simply translated.   Still, the work was done without much prejudice to the score; as all the numbers remained united to situations of a character similar to those for which they had been originally written.

What stands in the way of the music of "Fidelio" as regards the Parisian public is the chasteness of its melody; the great disdain of the composer for sonorous effects which are not justified; and his contempt for conventional terminations and periods which are too obvious. There is also additional cause in the opulent sobriety of his instrumentation; the boldness of his harmony; and, above all I venture to say, the profundity of his feeling for expression. Everything must be listened to in this complex music, everything must be *heard*, in order to enable us to understand it. The orchestral parts, which are sometimes principal and sometimes obscure, are liable to contain the very accent of expression, the cry of passion, in fact, the very idea; which the author may not have been able to give to the vocal part. This does not imply any lack of the latter's predominance; as those pretend who never tire of chanting the old reproaches. That addressed by Grétry to Mozart ran:

He has put the pedestal on the stage and the statue in the orchestra;

but the same had already been addressed to Gluck, and was, later on, addressed to Weber, Spontini and Beethoven. It will never cease to be addressed to any composer who abstains from writing platitudes for the voice, and who gives an interesting part to the orchestra; however much learning and discretion he may exhibit.

Truly, the people who are so prompt to blame the great masters for a pretended predominance of instruments over voices do not much esteem this learning or discretion; for we have seen, every day for the last ten years, the orchestra turned into a military band, a blacksmith's forge or a brazier's shop without this startling the critics or causing them to bestow upon these enormities the least attention. So that, on the whole, if the orchestra is noisy, violent, brutal, insipid, revolting and exterminating for voice and melody, the critics say nothing. But, if it is fine and intelligent—if it attracts a certain attention to itself by its vivacity, grace and eloquence—and if, notwithstanding all this, it still plays the part assigned to it by dramatic and musical exigence, it is blamed. The orchestra is easily pardoned either for saying nothing at all, or, should it speak, for uttering nothing but stupidity and coarseness.

There are sixteen numbers in the score of "Fidelio," without counting the four overtures. There were more in the original; some having been suppressed on the occasion of the second production at Vienna, besides which numerous cuts and modifications were made at the same time in the remaining numbers.

It was in 1855, I think, that a Leipzig editor decided to publish the complete original work; with indication of the cuts and changes which had been inflicted upon it. The study of this curious score gives an idea of the tortures which the impatient Beethoven was called upon to suffer in submitting to these revisions; which he did, no doubt, in a spirit of rage, and in comparing himself to the slave of Alfieri:

Servo, si, ma servo ognor fremente.

In Germany, as in Italy, as in France, as everywhere in the theatre; everybody, without exception, knows

better than the composer. The latter is a public enemy;
and, if a machine-boy thinks that such and such a
piece of music of any master is too long, everybody
will naturally consider him right against either Gluck,
Weber, Mozart, Rossini or Beethoven. See, with regard
to Rossini, the insolent suppressions made in his
"William Tell"; both before and after the first representation of that work of art. The theatre, for both
poets and musicians, is a school of humility; for poets
there get lessons from those who know nothing of
grammar, whilst musicians are taken in hand by those
who know nothing of the scale; and every Aristarch,
prejudiced moreover against anything which bears the
appearance of being new, or bold, is full of an in-
vincible love for the prudent and commonplace.

In the lyric theatres, especially, everybody takes upon
himself the right to apply the precept of Boileau:

Ajoutez quelquefois, et souvent effacez,

and they apply it so well, and in so many ways—some
of these correctors seeing black were others seeing
white—that a score which would have had some
fifty scenes, had it been let alone, will have some difficulty in issuing from their hands with as much as ten
pages intact.

The sixteen numbers of Beethoven's "Fidelio" have
all a beautiful and noble physiognomy. But they are
beautiful in different ways; and that is precisely what
appears to me to constitute their principle merit. The
first duet, between Marceline and her lover, is distin-

guished from the others by its style, which is familiar, gay and of a piquant simplicity; so that the character of the two personages is immediately revealed. The air in C minor of the young girl seems, in melodic form, to approach the style of the best samples of Mozart. The orchestra, however, is treated with a care more minute than was ever exercised by Beethoven's illustrious predecessor.

An exquisitely melodious quartet now follows. It is treated as a canon in the octave; each of the voices entering in turn to enounce the theme in such a way as to produce, first, a solo accompanied by a small orchestra of violoncellos, violas and clarinets; then, a duet, a trio and finally the quartet complete.

Rossini wrote a crowd of ravishing things in the same form, such as the canon in "Moïse":

Mi manca la voce.

But the canon of "Fidelio" is an andante, not followed by the perfunctory allegro, with *cabalette* and noisy coda; so that the public, although charmed by its graceful movement, remains surprised, and unable to make out why the allegro finale with its cadence, in fact its *whip-crack*, does not arrive. (By the by, why not really give it some whip-cracks?)

The couplets of Rocko on the power of gold, as written by Gaveaux in his French score, may now be compared to those in the German score by Beethoven. Of all the numbers in Gaveaux's opera this is, perhaps, the one best able to support such a comparison. Beethoven's melody has a jovial charm; the vigorous simplicity of which is varied in the middle by a modulation and a change of time. That of Gaveaux, though less elevated in style, has no less interest; this being due to its melodic frankness, the excellent diction of the words and a tasty orchestration.

In the following trio Beethoven begins to use a more spacious form, a vast development and an instrumentation more rich and agitated. We feel that we are now entering upon the real drama; the coming passion of which is revealed by distant lightning.

Afterwards appears a march, of which both melody and modulation are extremely attractive, although the general colour appears sad; as, however, might fairly be expected in a march of soldiers—the guardians of a prison. The two first notes of the theme, struck softly by the kettle-drums, with bass pizzicato, contribute at once to render it sombre. Neither this march nor the trio preceding it have any counterpart in the opera of Gaveaux; and the same may be said of many other numbers contained in Beethoven's rich score.

Amongst these may be reckoned the air of Pizarre; and although it receives no applause in Paris, we ask permission to treat it as a masterpiece. In this terrible number the ferocious joy of a monster about to satisfy his vengeance is painted with the most frightful truth. In his opera Beethoven has strictly observed Gluck's precept *not to employ instruments except in relation to the required degree of interest and passion.* Here, for the first time, the entire orchestra is unloosed; starting with fracas upon the chord of the minor ninth of D minor. Everything trembles and is agitated, whilst cries and blows abound; the vocal part being, it is true, a mere declamation. But, what a declamation! And what savage intensity its accent acquires when, after having established the major mode, the composer makes the chorus of guards intervene; whose voices, first murmuring in accompaniment to that of Pizarre, at last break out with force at the conclusion! It is admirable!

I have heard this air sung in Germany, in overpowering fashion, by Pischek.

The duet between Rocko and the governor, which is of course for two basses, is not quite up to this level; but, still, I cannot approve of the liberty they took at the Theâtre-Lyrique in suppressing it.

A similar liberty, though one taken with the consent (more or less real) of the composer, was that which happened at Vienna in the case of the charming duet for soprani, sung by Fidelio and Marceline; in which one violin and one violoncello, aided by a few orchestral entries, accompany the two voices with such elegance. This duet, being found in the Leipzig score of which I spoke just now, has been reinstated in Beethoven's work, at the Theâtre-Lyrique. The wiseacres of the Paris theatre, accordingly, do not agree with those of Vienna! How fortunate that there should be divergence of opinion among them! But for that, we should have been prevented from ever hearing this musical dialogue—so fresh, so sweet and elegant!

It is to the prompter of the Theâtre-Lyrique, they say, that we owe this re-installation. Bravo, prompter!

The great air of "Fidelio" is with *recitative, adagio cantabile* and *allegro-finale*; being accompanied by three horns and one bassoon *obbligati.*

I find the *recitative* a fine dramatic movement; the adagio sublime by its tender accent and melancholy grace; the allegro exciting, full of a noble enthusiasm and magnificent, even to the degree of being well worthy to have served as model for the air of Agathe in "Der Freischütz." I know that excellent critics are not of my opinion; but I am quite happy not to be of theirs.

The theme of the allegro of this admirable air is proposed by the three horns and the bassoon alone; who confine themselves to sounding, successively, the five notes—

B, E, G, B, E,

which occupies four bars of incredible originality. You might give these five notes to any musician who does not know them, and I bet that, in a hundred combinations, there will not be found one to equal the proud and impetuous phrase which Beethoven has drawn from them; so entirely unforeseen is the rhythm employed. This allegro strikes many people as having one great fault; it does not contain any little phrase that they can easily remember. These amateurs, insensible to the numerous and striking beauties of this number, look out for their four-bar phases just like children look out for the prize in a Twelfth-cake; or like people in the country look out for the high B, when a new tenor appears. The cake might be exquisite and the tenor the most delightful singer in the world; but neither one nor the other would have any success:

There's no prize inside that cake!
Where's his high note?

The air of Agathe in "Der Freischütz" is almost popular: but, then, it *has the note*! How many pieces, even by Rossini, that prince of melodists, have remained in the shade; because *they lacked the note*!

The four wind instruments which accompany the voice in this air somewhat annoy most listeners by attracting too much of their, attention. These instruments, however, make no display of useless difficulties. Beethoven has not treated them as Mozart frequently did the basset-horn; as *solo* instruments, that is, in the pretentious acceptation of the term. Mozart, in "Tito," gives a kind of "concerto" to the basset-horn, whilst the *prima donna* is singing *that she sees death advancing*, etc. This contrast of one personage who is animated by sentiments of the saddest kind with a virtuose who, under the pretence of accompanying her song, thinks of nothing but showing off the agility of his fingers, is one of the most disgraceful,

puerile, contrary to dramatic good sense, and even one
of the most unfavourable to good musical effect. The
part entrusted by Beethoven to his four wind instruments is not of this kind. There is no question of
displaying them, but of obtaining an accompaniment
in perfect accord with the sentiment of the character
who is singing; and, for that purpose, a special sonority which no other orchestral combination could
produce.

The tone of the horns, which is somewhat veiled and
even painful, blends perfectly with the mournful joy
and uneasy hope with which the heart of Leonora is
filled. It is as sweet and tender as the cooing of
doves; and, towards the same period, Spontini, without having heard Beethoven's "Fidelio," employed the
horns with a very similar intention in accompanying
that beautiful air of the "Vestale":

Toi que j'implore.

Several masters since then, Donizetti amongst the
rest in his "Lucia," have paid Beethoven the same
compliment.

Such is the evidence of the expressive force peculiar
to this instrument, in certain cases; when used by composers familiar with the musical language of passion
and sentiment. It was certainly a great and tender
soul whose feeling was reflected in this moving
inspiration!

The emotion caused by the chorus of prisoners, no
less poignant, is quite as profound.

A troop of unfortunates issue from their dungeons and come for a moment to breathe the open air in the prison square. Listen, as they enter, to those first few bars of the orchestra; to those sweet and broad harmonies which seem to open out so radiantly; and to those timid voices which group slowly but at last arrive at a harmonic expansion which seems to be exhaled from those breasts so habitually oppressed; precisely like a sigh of happiness. And that melodious design which accompanies them! One might say again here:

Why did the composer not give the melodic design to the voices, and the vocal parts to the orchestra?

Why? Because it would have been an evident clumsiness. The voices sing precisely as they ought to sing. One note more placed in the vocal parts would spoil the justness and truth of an expression which has been profoundly felt. The instrumental design is only a secondary idea, however melodious it may be, and it particularly suits the wind instruments and brings out the sweetness of the vocal harmonies, so ingeniously disposed above the orchestra, to perfection. No composer of good sense could, I believe, be found (no matter what school he might belong to) to disapprove of Beethoven's idea in this case.

The happiness of the prisoners is disturbed, for a moment, by the appearance of the guards deputed to watch them. Immediately the musical colour changes; everything becomes gloomy and dull. But the guards have finished their round; their suspicious glance has ceased to weigh upon the captives. Accordingly, the tonality of the episodial passage of the chorus gradually approaches that of the principal key : nearer and nearer it comes; the key is touched; then, a short silence. And, now, the first theme appears in the primitive key so entrancingly true to nature that I will not venture even to try to give an idea of it. It is the light; it is the air; sweet liberty—life—which is given back to us.

Some listeners, drying their eyes at the end of this chorus, are indignant at the silence, feeling that the place should echo again with an immense acclamation. It is possible that the greater part of the public are really moved; but there are, nevertheless, certain kinds of musical beauty, evident to all, and yet which are not calculated to excite applause.

The prisoners' chorus in the opera by Gaveaux :

Que ce beau ciel, cette verdure,

is written in the same sentiment; but, alas ! compared with that of Beethoven, it appears *very* gloomy and flat. Let us, moreover, remark that the French composer, who is very careful about employing his trombones in all the rest of his score, chooses to let them intervene in this place; precisely as if they belonged to the family of instruments possessed of a timbre sweet, calm and suave. Let whoever can explain this strange fancy.

In the second part of the duet. where Rocko tells Fidelio that they are going together to dig the prisoner's grave, there is a syncopated design for wind instruments, the effect of which is very strange; but, by its sighing rhythm and uneasy movement, perfectly adapted to the situation. This duet and the quintet following contain some very fine passages, of which a few approach, as far as the style of the vocal parts is concerned, Mozart's manner in the "Marriage of Figaro."

A quintet, with chorus, concludes this act. In this piece, the colour of which is very properly sombre, a somewhat dry modulation appears brusquely about half-way through; and some of the voices execute rhythms distinguishable from others, but without its appearing very clearly what was the intention of the composer. The mystery, however, which reigns over the ensemble gives to this finale a most dramatic physiognomy; and it finishes *piano*, expressive of consternation and fear. So the Parisian public does not applaud it; not being able to applaud a conclusion so contrary to its usual habits.

Before the rise of the curtain for the third act the orchestra performs a slow and lugubrious symphony full of long cries of anguish, sobs, tremblings and heavy pulsations. We are about to enter upon the scene of pain and grief; Florestan is outstretched upon his bed of straw; and we are to be present at his agony —to hear his cries of delirium.

The orchestration of Gluck for the dungeon scene of Oreste in "Iphigenia in Tauride" is very beautiful, no doubt; but to what a height does Beethoven here soar above his rival! Not merely because he is an immense symphonist, or because he knows better how to make the orchestra speak; but—and it is important to remember it—because his musical thought in this number is stronger, grander and infinitely more penetrating. We feel, from the very first bars, that the unfortunate occupant of that dungeon must, on entering it, have *left all hope behind him.*

The following is the description. A mournful recitative, interspersed by the principal phrases of the preceding symphony, is succeeded by a desolate and heartrending cantabile; the sadness of which is increased at every instant by the accompaniment of the wind instruments. The grief of the prisoner becomes more and more intense. His brain wanders; for the wing of death has touched him. Seized by a sudden hallucination he thinks that he is free; he smiles, while tears of tenderness roll down from his dying eyes; he imagines that he sees his wife again, that he calls and that she answers; he is intoxicated with the thought of liberty and love.

To others must fall the task of worthily depicting this melody of sobs; these palpitations of the orchestra; the faithful song of the oboe, which follows that of Florestan like the voice of the adored spouse which he thinks he hears; that exciting *crescendo* and the last cry of the dying man. I cannot do it.

Here let us recognise the sovereign art, the burning inspiration and the electric flight of genius.

Florestan has fallen back upon his couch after this fit of febrile agitation; and Rocko now comes, accompanied by the trembling Leonora (Fidelio).

The terror of this scene dwindles in the new libretto; which makes it a mere question of clearing out a cistern, instead of digging the grave of a prisoner who is still alive. (That will show you what "improvements" lead to.)

There could be nothing more sinister than this celebrated duet, in which the cold insensibility of Rocko is in contrast with the heartrending asides of Fidelio, and in which the dull murmur of the orchestra might be compared to the dead sound of earth falling upon a coffin which is being covered. One of our critical confrères has very justly referred to a resemblance between this number and the scene of the grave-diggers in "Hamlet." He could have afforded it any higher praise.

The grave-diggers of Beethoven finish their duet, without any coda. They have also no *cabalette* and no vocal demonstration of any kind; for which reason the pit preserves, in their respect, a rigorous silence. You see where the trouble is!

The trio which follows is more fortunate; for it receives applause, although it has a quiet ending. Its three characters, being animated by affectionate sentiments, have suave melodies to sing; and these are sustained, without strain or effort, by extremely harmonious accompaniments. Nothing could be more touching and at the same time more elegant than the beautiful theme of twenty bars delivered by the tenor. This is "song" in its most exquisite purity; this is "expression," in its truest, simplest and most far-reaching form. This theme is afterwards resumed; sometimes in its entirety, sometimes by fragments; and, after some bold modulations, it is brought back to the original key with incomparable skill and effect.

The pistol-quartet is one long roll of thunder, the threatening character of which continually increases, and which concludes with a series of explosions. After the cry of Fidelio: "I am his wife!" the musical and dramatic interests are no longer distinguishable apart. The hearer is moved, excited or disturbed without being able to decide whether his violent emotion is due to the voices, the instruments or the dramatic action; to such a striking degree of truth and with such prodigious energy has the composer identified himself with the situation depicted. The voices, challenging one another and replying in heated apostrophes, are always heard amidst the tumult of the orchestra; and, across this feature, we hear the strings; like the vociferations of a crowd, agitated by a thousand passions. It is a miracle of dramatic music, for which I know of no counterpart in any master; either ancient or modern.

The changing of the libretto has inflicted enormous and most regrettable injury upon this beautiful scene. As the action had been transferred to a period when the pistol had not yet been invented, they were obliged to forego giving it to Fidelio as an offensive weapon. The young woman, accordingly, threatens Pizarre only with an iron bar; which is incomparably less dangerous, and especially for such a man, than the little tube with which even a feeble hand could have struck him dead upon making the least movement. Moreover, the very gesture of Fidelio, taking aim at the face of Pizarre imparts a grand scenic effect. I can still see Madame Devrient, stretching out her trembling arm in the direction of Pizarre, and laughing with a convulsive laugh.

That is what results from this bungling of scores and texts; which are supposed to be thus accommodated to what the public demands. The public demands nothing at all; and would only be too pleased to have certain works offered to it exactly in the condition in which they were written by their authors.

After this admirable quartet the couple, being left alone, sing a duet of equal excellence; in which intense passion, joy, surprise and depression borrow in turn from the music an expression of which it would be impossible to convey an idea to anyone who has not heard it. What love! transports! fervour! with what passion these two beings embrace one another! How they stammer for very earnestness! The words crowd up to their trembling lips; they stagger; they are breathless—in short, *they love*! Realise that well; for all comes from the fact that they truly love.

What is there in common between such transports of affection and the insipid duets of those who have been united by a mere conventional marriage?

In the last finale we have an extensive concerted number, the march rhythm of which is first interrupted by a few episodial slow movements; the allegro is then resumed, and proceeds with continually increasing animation and sonority, right on to the end. In this peroration the coldest and most stubborn listeners are dazzled and captivated; by its majesty, in the first place; but also by its extraordinary life. That is when they put on an air of gracious approval; saying:

Not so bad!

Seeing them applaud we may fairly repeat their gracious observation; and say, also:

Not so bad!

But, then, all the rest of the score, though it touches them so little, is none the less admirable for that; and, without wishing to depreciate this gigantic finale, several of the preceding numbers are superior and even *much* superior to it.

Yet, who knows whether light may not come sooner than we expect; even to those whose hearts are closed at present to this fine work of Eeethoven, as they are also closed at present to the Ninth Symphony, the last quartets, and the great piano sonatas of this incomparable master? A thick veil seems to be sometimes placed before the mind's eye as it glances towards one particular region of the heavenly expanse of art. It is thus prevented from perceiving the great planets by which that portion is illumined. But, all at once, from some unknown cause, the veil is torn away. Then, at last, we see; and blush to have been so long blind.

This thought reminds me of poor Adolphe Nourrit. He declared to me one day that, in the whole of Shakespeare's works, he found only "Macbeth" to admire; and that he regarded "Hamlet," in particular, as unintelligible and absurd. Three years afterwards he came to me; saying, with the emotion of concentrated enthusiasm:

Hamlet is the masterpiece of the greatest philosophic poet who ever lived. I understand it now. My heart and head are filled with it; for it intoxicates me. You must have had a singular opinion of my poetic sense and intelligence. Give me back your esteem.

Alas! poor Yorick!

BEETHOVEN IN THE RING OF SATURN.

BEETHOVEN IN THE RING OF SATURN.

(THE MEDIUMS.)

THE whole musical world seems, for the moment, to be very much moved; the entire philosophy of art is completely upset. Up to a few days ago the general belief was that the beautiful in music, just the same as the indifferent and ugly, was "absolute." By this is meant that a piece which was either beautiful or commonplace or ugly in the estimation of those people who are supposed to be gifted with taste, as well as connoisseurs generally, was sure to be equally beautiful, commonplace or ugly for everybody else; including those who were unpossessed of either taste or knowledge. The result of this consoling opinion was that a masterpiece capable of bringing tears to the eyes of an inhabitant of No. 58 Rue de la Chaussée d'Autin, Paris, or of boring him, or revolting him, as the case might happen to be, was bound to produce the same effect upon a Cochin Chinese, or a

Laplander, or a Timor-pirate, or a Turk, or upon a
street-porter living in "Naughty-word Street."* When I
say that the *general belief* was such, I mean amongst
scholars, doctors, and the single-hearted; because, in
these questions, great and little minds come together
in one way or other; either by resembling one another
or by meeting together.† As to me, considering that
I happen to be neither scholar, doctor nor simple, I
have never been quite able to fix my opinion about
these grave subjects of controversy. However, my
present opinion is that I have never had any opinion;
in fact, I am now so sure of that that I have become
perfectly settled in believing in the absolutely beautiful no more than I do in the horn of the unicorn. But,
besides that, let me ask you: "Why not believe in
the horn of the unicorn?" It is now superlatively
proved that there *are* unicorns in several parts of the
Himalayas. Take the adventures of Mr. Kingsdoom.
That celebrated English traveller, astonished to meet
with one of these animals, which he had previously
thought to be fabulous (you see now what believing
comes to!), and, looking at it with an attention by
which the elegant quadruped felt hurt, was suddenly
pounced upon by the irritated creature, which nailed
him against a tree, leaving a long piece of his horn
fixed in the traveller's breast, by way of proving his

---

* Rue des Mauvaises-Paroles.
† Qui ne se ressemble pas s'assemble.

existence. The poor Englishman was unable to get over it.

I must now give the reason why I have recently become so fixed in the view that I can no longer believe in the absolutely beautiful in music. A revolution must have taken place, and really *has* taken place in philosophy, since the marvellous discovery of table-turning (deal tables); and consequently of mediums; and consequently of the evocation of spirits; and consequently of spirit-conversations. Music could not remain outside the influence of such an important fact. It could not remain isolated from the world of spirits: music, the science of the impalpable; imponderable; and of the indiscernible.

A good many musicians have therefore placed themselves into relation of the spirit-world (they ought to have done it long ago). By means of a deal table, costing very little, on which the hands are placed, and which, after a few minutes reflection (reflection by the table) starts lifting one or two of its legs in such a way, unfortunately, as to shock the delicacy of the English ladies, they succeed, not only in calling up the spirit of a great composer, but even in entering into regular conversation with him, and in forcing him to reply to all sorts of questions.

More than that. By diligent application it is possible to compel the spirit of the great master to dictate a new work; an entire composition, proceeding directly from his brain.

The same as for the letters of the alphabet it is agreed that the table, in lifting its legs, and in letting them fall again, gives so many strokes for C; so many for D; so many for F; so many for a crotchet; so many for a quaver; so many for one rest; so many for another; and so on.

I know what you are about to answer me: "It is agreed, you tell us. Agreed with whom? It must have been with the spirits. But, before this convention was established, how did the first medium go to work in order to come to an agreement with the spirits?"

I cannot tell you. The only thing that is sure is that it is all quite sure; and, in such great question, you must be absolutely guided by your interior sense, and not meet trouble half way. *Now, already, therefore* (as the Russians say), they have lately called up the spirit of Beethoven; who lives in Saturn. Mozart lives in Jupiter; but everybody knows that. It seems as if the author of "Fidelio" ought really to have chosen the same planet for his new residence; but Beethoven is known to be a little rough and capricious, and he might even entertain some unavowed antipathy for Mozart. So it happens that he dwells in Saturn; or, rather, in Saturn's ring. And thus it came to pass that, on Monday last, a medium who was on extra good terms with the great man, and was not afraid of putting him into a bad humour by making him take such a long voyage for nothing at all, placed his hands on the deal table for the purpose of sending to Beethoven, in Saturn's ring, the order to come and talk with him for a moment.

At once the table began to make indecent movements; to lift its legs and to show—well, to show that the spirit was near. The poor spirits, we must admit, are very obedient. Beethoven, whilst he was on earth, would not have put himself out of the way to go even from the Porte de Carinthie to the Imperial Palace even if the Emperor of Austria had sent to beg him urgently to come. And now he quits Saturn's ring, and 'interrupts his high contemplations to obey the *order* (mark the word) of the very first comer who only happens to be possessed of a deal table.

See the effect of death and how that changes your character!

Marmontel was quite right when he said in his opera of "Zémiry et Azor":

Les esprits, dont on nous fait peur
Sont les meilleures gens du monde.

And so it is. But you will remember that I told you in such questions not to meet trouble half way.

So Beethoven arrives; and, by means of the legs of the table, he says:

"Here I am!"

The medium, delighted, thereupon gives him a familiar tap. "Come! come!" you will say to me. "Now you are letting off a few absurdities."

"Bah!"

"Yes, indeed you are. You were just now talking about the spirits' 'brain'; and, as spirits have no bodies, they can have no brains."

"No, no, no, you understand they are—they are— well that has already been explained. They are *semi-bodies*. And, please don't interrupt me any more with such futile observations, and allow me to continue my sad story."

Well, the medium (who is himself a *semi-spirit*) gives a *semi-blow* on some *semi-fraction* of Beethoven's apparatus; and, without the least ado, asks the *semi-god* to dictate a new sonata.

Beethoven does not wait to be asked twice; so the table begins to frisk about and the sonata is written under the composer's own dictation. This done, Beethoven returns to Saturn; and the medium, surrounded by a dozen wondering spectators, approaches the piano and executes the sonata. The same "wondering spectators" are now quickly transformed into "puzzled listeners"; for there is no mistake about the sonata in the sense that it is *no semi-piece of nonsense*. It is, on the contrary, a fine full-blown piece of nonsense; not to say of utter stupidity.

How can we believe, after that, in the absolutely beautiful? Certainly Beethoven, in going to inhabit a superior world, could but perfect himself. His genius could only increase and become more elevated; so that, in dictating a new sonata, he must have intended to give the inhabitants of earth some idea of the new style he has adopted in his new residence; an idea of his

Fourth Period;

an idea of the kind of music they play upon the Erards in Saturn's ring. And, to think that this new style is precisely what the petty musicians of a petty sub-Saturian world call the stupid style; the worthless or insupportable style; and, far from causing them to feel ravished to the fifty-eighth heaven, it makes them sick, and would be enough to drive them out of their minds—that is if they had any to be driven out of.

For the same reason we are bound to believe that, as neither the beautiful nor the ugly is universal, a good many productions of the human mind which are admired on earth will not be thought much of in the spirit-world; and I feel justified in concluding (by the way I have had no doubt of it for a long time) that certain operas, which are every day represented and applauded, even at theatres which delicacy forbids me to name, will be hissed off the stage in Saturn, Jupiter, Mars, Venus, Pallas, Sirrus, Neptune, the great and little Bears, and the Wagon constellation; being in short, nothing but infinite platitudes for the infinite universe.

This conviction is not exactly calculated to encourage the great producers. Several of them have been quite overcome by the fatal discovery; and, having fallen ill in consequence of it, are likely enough (so they say) to shortly join the world of spirits.

Luckily, that will be for a long time.

University of Illinois Press
1325 South Oak Street
Champaign, IL 61820-6903
www.press.uillinois.edu